To Mora–

The Sunny Side Up!

Keep shining;

The Sunny Girl,

The Sunny Side Up!

The Sunny Girl,
Lauren Cook

iUniverse, Inc.
Bloomington

The Sunny Side Up!

iUniverse books may be ordered through booksellers or by contacting:

iUniverse
1663 Liberty Drive
Bloomington, IN 47403
www.iuniverse.com
1-800-Authors (1-800-288-4677)

ISBN: 978-1-4759-8187-2 (sc)
ISBN: 978-1-4759-8188-9 (e)

Printed in the United States of America

iUniverse rev. date: 04/18/2013

"Like Stars Across the Sky
We Were Born to Shine
Because We Believe."
-Andrea Bocelli

Keep Shining

Contents

The Sunny Start Up

Happiness. You'd be surprised how often the word is said in every day conversation if you listen for it. But with this one word comes hundreds of meanings. Happiness is not just the pursuit our founding fathers wrote about or the moment we fall in love; it's what we want for the basis of our lives. It is an overarching dream yet it is also a hope for our day-to-day living. It is a commonplace goal that we all strive for and humbly hope for.

The good news is that happiness is everywhere if you look for it. It's that split-second when your iPod plays the perfect song on shuffle, it's when your mom makes that macaroni and cheese you've been missing, and it's when you've finally met a best friend who *just gets you*. With so many opportunities for unearthed happiness, shouldn't we learn how to discover it? We may not always recognize it or appreciate it, but I believe that we are hardwired for happiness. We just need to take the time to treasure it. I'm here to help you notice those yet-to-be-seized moments more often, and to help you appreciate them more on a daily basis.

Sure, we're hearing the word "happiness" all the time, but are we actually feeling it? Furthermore, are we looking for it in the right places? An article in *Psychological Science* recently reported that contrary to popular opinion, especially in America, happiness does not look like a new Ferrari or a Coach clutch. Novelty purchases can be great things, but the satisfaction is fleeting. Momentary happiness does not mean that it's *meaningful* happiness. That hot, red paint fades on the car and the purse goes out of fashion in three months. Instead, I'm looking at a happiness that will always have its engine running and that will never go out of style. It comes from your soul, not your wallet.

I'm talking about a happiness that you can't always touch; an inner joy and a sense of gratitude that somehow makes even the little things in your life become a source of happiness. Maybe it's in the perfect grasp of a tender hand, or the sound of innocent laughter from your baby cousin playing outside. It's in the smile of your best friend or in the eyes of your wise grandma. It's in the hug from your mom after a long day or it's in a playful nudge from your beloved family pet. Happiness comes from our relationships with people; it's not from our relationship with material goods. Once we start cultivating these connections, we can truly start living a life of happiness.

So why now? Why is today the perfect day for you start striving for happiness? In a world where it is often cool to be "too cool" for enthusiasm and nonchalance becomes the norm, a positive attitude has never been more necessary. It's time to be proud of being happy. Share your smile with everyone you know. Taking charge of your happiness will give you a passion for life that until now may have been untapped. Your compassion for others will increase tenfold, your goals to give back and to make something of yourself will kick into high gear, and you'll feel that you are truly reaping the benefits of what this life has to offer.

Some might say that happiness is something that *happens* to you. I beg to differ. Happiness is something that you can *have*; you just have to want it enough. It is all yours for the taking. Of course happiness may dawn on us at different times, but it is often a deliberate mentality. You can decide to find the positive in even the most stressful situations if you are willing. Happiness doesn't occur by chance—you can choose it for yourself. So with your decision in favor of happiness, it's time to get excited—because with this positive attitude comes the great desire to make a difference, to be a more productive person, and to love others in a way that was previously unattainable. You may see the world in a completely new light. Your life is about to change for the better—I know that mine did once I became conscious of my happiness.

Everyone deserves happiness. As you yearn for it for your life, you will long to share it with others. Being happy is not something to hide, even though naysayers may stick their nose up to it. They're missing out! Just because someone wants to hold back on the potential for an outstandingly happy life doesn't mean that you should. I know that it can sometimes seem like "happy people" can be obnoxious or overrated, but it's time to put that point to rest. Because the truth is, happy people lead healthier and more fulfilling lives, no matter what their external circumstances may be. This is because happy people know that long lasting happiness isn't in their material possessions—it's in their meaningful relationships. So no matter what you look like or how much money you have, it won't mean much if you don't have inner happiness fueling your life. Anyone can be happy and it starts with loving what you do and loving the people with whom you spend your time. As the cover says, it all starts with giving back, giving thanks, and giving love in your relationships. I know you can do that!

I'm writing this book because I want happiness for your life. I want you to capitalize on the moments when you've experienced sheer joy, and increase that abundantly in your day-to-day life. I want to help you develop an appreciation for what you've been given and an aspiration for where you'd like to go. No dream is too big, no fear is too unconquerable, and no amount of happiness is too much to ask for in your life.

People often ask me how I came up with the idea of "The Sunny Girl" brand. It was a bunch of little things but it ultimately came to one undeniable word that kept permeating into my life: "happiness." It's already been written 28 times in these three pages alone. As I have come to learn, we need to put happiness into the forefront of our consciousness. It's more than just something to hope for in the future, we need to believe that happiness can be had in the here and now. So many of us say that one of the most important goals is to "just be happy" *someday* but how often do we describe ourselves as such currently? Are we *actually* happy people—or are we just hoping to be happy *one day*?

I realized that I was one of these people; hoping to be happy at some point in my life. Whenever that point was, I had no idea. Happiness would come when I got in to college, when I landed the dream job, when I found my perfect match. But I realized with my study on happiness that happiness doesn't have to be a landing mark or a momentary feeling; happiness can be a general sense of well-being no matter where I am in my life.

I wanted to write this book specifically with a young adult audience in mind (although I think the information is valuable at any age) because we are embarking on some of the most important decisions in our lives— where we want to go to college, who we want to date, what we want to study, and where we want to work. These decisions are often some of the most consequential choices we will make and they impact us for the rest of our lives. Starting at a young age, when lifelong habits are forming, we need to get in the habit of happiness.

If we don't use our own happiness as a guide, we may get trapped into someone else's happiness, like our parents' or society's for that matter. I remember Gretchen Rubin's book, *The Happiness Project* and reading about her epiphany at 40. Instead of searching for happiness during her young adult life, she had to detour and alter her way of living long after she had settled into a career she was dissatisfied with. While every path has value, my intention with this book is to serve as a preventative measure for the mid life crisis. We should do what makes us happy at the starting gate—not at the halfway point.

If you're just like the rest of us, trying to find your way in the world, this book is for you. It was written for you, by many of you. This book is hundreds of heads put together in one inclusive piece, offering many perspectives, attitudes, ideas and emotions. I interviewed hundreds of teens, college students, and young adults to get the most representative sample of what happiness means to us. As Henry Wadsworth Longfellow said, "The human voice is the organ of the soul," so I hope you will find your peers' words to be meaningful. You should also know that all the names have been changed—the responses are anonymous—but they all still hold the same inspiration, wisdom, and honesty that needs to be shared.

With so many opinions and ideas, I composed the book in to 12 categories, all of which contribute to our overall happiness. People voluntarily wrote about what it was in their life that brought them the most joy—whether it was their spirituality, their relationship with their family, or their avid love for a particular hobby or activity. Happiness is different for everyone but it is my hope that you can take away an expansive view of happiness and apply it to your life. Happiness is everywhere, you just have to be receptive to it.

Because this book is a collaborative effort, within each chapter you'll find that I've included "Sunny Samples" featuring quotes from others who have contributed. I'll also share my best "Sunny Suggestions" giving you concrete tips about how you can increase happiness in your life. Some of these ideas may recommend that you take a few extra minutes to write down various goals and concepts—I think this would be highly beneficial for you. Just like with all events in life, the benefits you get depend on the effort you are willing to put in. It is one thing to read over the tips but it is entirely different when you apply these Sunny Suggestions to your own life. Get personal with yourself in these pages and take those extra minutes to write. Sometimes it's not until we've put the pen to the paper that we can discover new things about ourselves.

This book is designed as the guidance we have needed and the camaraderie we have craved as young adults. It represents who we are as a generation and how we can find happiness in this era. We are living in a unique time of rapid change and in this day of tweets, tags, texts, and the like, happiness has never been more essential to our well-being. Unlike the mechanics and technology that govern so much of our world, individual and shared happiness is a human experience now and always. This book caters specifically to the need for human connection to create happiness—despite our computer-crazed culture. No matter how advanced society becomes, at the end of the day, happiness will always be about and between people.

Another reason I've been inspired to write this book is because I want to help us stay in the present. So often I hear people say, "I can't wait for the weekend," "I can't wait to graduate," or "I can't wait to turn 21." I'm guilty of it myself sometimes. Do you see the problem with this? When we're wishing our time away, soon, there won't be much of it left. Before we know it we'll be turning, 30, 40, then shock, 50. We'll be *wishing* for those days of study nights with our friends, classes that we were actually interested in, and yes, looking younger than 21. You can only live your life once—so let's live it right the first time with no regrets. It's time to seize YOUR day—to not wish your time away, because truly, you can never get today back. Let's make each day count!

With every page, I am keeping your happiness ever at heart. I want you to experience your life with the utter joy that you deserve but I also want to offer you a little extra sunshine when you've been in a spell of rainy days, because the truth is, life isn't always sunflowers. We'll find that life isn't about riches, fame, and fortune as our celebrity centered society tries to sell us. Instead, life is about living out a richly wonderful journey filled with meaningful relationships and expansive adventures that help you break away from your barriers. Opening this book is just the start of that.

Keep shining,

The Sunny Girl, Lauren Cook

The Hunt for Happiness

What does happiness mean to you? It might be something tangible, like that Gold-Medal Ribbon scoop from Baskin Robbins that you've been getting since you were five, or maybe it's that kiss you had under your doorstep last night. Maybe it's more of a feeling, like that sense of peace you have as you drift off in to a slumber or the mindless rhythm of a good run. It can be a million little things and it can be one overarching feeling of complete contentment.

Your Sunny Side: What does happiness mean to you?

I asked hundreds of young adults this question and no two people gave the same answer. Everyone had their own unique perspective on happiness. But naturally, being the college student that I am, I wanted to include a dictionary definition of the word happiness before we spice it up a bit. Here's what happiness is, according to Merriman Webster: "a good fortune, a pleasurable or satisfying experience, and a state of well-being and contentment." A little boring, right? Happiness is much too good of a word to be defined in such a plain-Jane way. When I asked myself the same question, "What does happiness mean to me?" I realized the answer wasn't so simple. I've studied happiness for over two years now—I've written about it, talked about it, blogged about it and I've delved into this complex topic with a sincere curiosity and an intense interest, yet still, putting happiness in a one-sentence definition just doesn't quite do the word justice.

But because you've pinned me down at this point, here's **My Sunny Side**. Happiness is a feeling, either temporary or long lasting, that gives one a sense of peace, excitement, or joy. Side effects include, but are not limited to, smiling, hugging, laughing, sharing, and the occasional bout of singing and dancing. It may not always be a choice but it can be a perspective, even in the face of challenging external circumstances.

In all seriousness though, happiness doesn't have to be larger-than-life with the big band playing and the flash mob gathering like you're at Disneyland. It can be simple, pure, and momentary, or it can be a prolonged feeling that is nearly indescribable but still very present—both are powerful and both are something that we should hold on to in our lives. Happiness is a gift but what's special about this gift is that while others can give it to us, we can also give it to ourselves. No matter how we receive it, the important thing is that we are thankful for it each time we experience it and that we bestow it upon others so they may enjoy it just as much as we have.

The most insightful thing I have learned about happiness is that the more places I look for it, the more places I find it. Even though these places may change depending on where I am in my life, there are always new places to look. Sometimes, it's seeing a beautiful new flower on my way to work (sunflowers are my favorite in case you couldn't tell). Sometimes it's taking a catnap with my cat who I sometimes think has a better understanding of life than I do. It could be the perfect date or being told that I'm loved. Happiness is always there in laughter. Even though some may think regular bouts of happiness are unobtainable, I've found that happiness isn't in hiding—it wants to be found just as much as we want to find it. We just have to look in the right places. Here are a few ideas on where to start looking.

Sunny Samples

1. Savannah: "Happiness is when you are loving what you have, loving yourself, and loving how your life is."

2. Christie: "Happiness is anything or anyone that can put a smile on your face. A baby giggling, a slumber party, a trip to Rome, a good grade, anything that makes you feel proud."

3. Jim: "Happiness is just a mindset. When I set my mind on being happy about doing something, I am happy doing it. That's what it really boils down to but it took me a long time to discover that."

4. Allison: "Honestly, I believe that happiness comes from the things we take for granted, the things that pass under our radar. When we take the time to notice the good things, instead of focusing on all the bad, we will naturally be happier."

5. Kevin: "It is being healthy both physically and emotionally. It is surrounding myself with people that treat me with respect and love. It is respecting myself by taking a step back and thinking about my options. It is being able to wake up in the morning and know that today is a new day."

6. Kara: "I think happiness is about going to sleep at night and being content with the person that you are and the path you are on."

7. Jacob: "Happiness is a universal want and need. It means making the best out of what you have and not settling for anything less than what you are capable of. Happiness comes when you make it happen."

8. Collin: "Happiness means that I'm in a state where I am completely immersed in the present. Where time flies, where I have no conception of anything past or future and I revel in the moment."

9. Kimberly: "Happiness means that you are in a moment or a place in your life that you are consciously enjoying. I like to pause during the day and realize how happy I am and how everything happens for a reason. I love embracing the imperfections of life—it just makes it more interesting."

10. Stephanie: "Happiness is surrounding yourself with the people and things that give you the most joy. It's loving yourself so much that negative

thoughts cannot produce a negative outlook. It's being so comfortable and self-aware that you don't feel the need to compare. It's not sweating the small stuff and it's living a simple life. It's not taking yourself too seriously."

Sunny Suggestion

On a daily basis we engage in a lot of small talk. This week, I encourage you to **have a real conversation about what happiness means to you**. Find out what makes your friends and family happy and share with them what makes you truly happy. We often keep our thoughts on happiness to ourselves, but it's time to go beyond the small talk and share something deeper.

Your Sunny Side: How does your family define happiness?

_____

_____

How do your friends define happiness?

_____

_____

Learning Your Sunny Score

When I asked young adults how happy they were on a scale of one to ten, I'll be honest, I was expecting low scores. Even I had fallen prey to the stereotype that teenagers and young adults were unhappy. But I was proven wrong—blatantly wrong. And I couldn't be happier about that.

When I asked the research question, "How happy are you?" it was not to ask how they were feeling that day or what they hoped to feel eventually.

It was meant to assess their everyday baseline level of happiness. Using a pool of over 300 survey responses, there were very few that scored below a six, in fact the average score was a solid eight.

My Sunny Side

What's my score? I'd say I'm at a solid eight or nine. I think we certainly have our temporary "10's" but I don't think they can last forever. Quite frankly, I don't think it's realistic. Those moments of sheer bliss are magical but they are usually momentary. Can you imagine if we went through life skipping to class and singing at the dinner table? Without a little bit of ho-hum in our lives, we'd never truly appreciate our moments of genuine happiness. Besides, sometimes when we're faced with distress or sadness, we are motivated to search for answers and ultimately learn more about ourselves. Feeling sad isn't something to be ashamed of; while it's important to strive for happiness, it's also important to allow ourselves to feel how we want and need to feel in our most distressing moments. It's healthy. Letting those darker emotions come to you isn't a bad thing, but when you suppress them or let them linger for a prolonged period of time it can block your happiness.

Yet even on a bad day, I like to think that I am a very happy person. I'm not ecstatic every waking moment of every day but I generally feel light of heart. For me, my happiness score goes up when I'm actively "doing." When I'm *doing* writing, *doing* dancing--*doing* life. It's when I'm with people who are just as passionate about life as I am. I love to make people laugh and I love it even more when people make me laugh. Happiness is when I'm saying "yes" to the right things and saying "no" to the wrong things. It's when I'm noticing my world and I'm deciding to actively be a part of it. But trust me, even though I'm "The Sunny Girl," I don't eat sunshine for breakfast and the birds and bunnies don't follow me when I walk to class. I'm a real person; some days are great, some are good and some are downright horrible. But no matter what kind of day I'm having, I try to focus on bringing happiness into each one. I am confident that you can do the same after you've read this book.

Sunny Suggestion

Normally I place the Sunny Suggestions at the end of a section but I don't want to create a bias, so let's check your baseline before we begin. Give yourself your own Sunny Score. Try not to figure your score on your momentary feeling as you read this. Instead, center your score on your natural demeanor through everyday life. Do you find yourself smiling often, or do you catch yourself with a frown? What do you think?

Your Sunny Side Score: _____

Why would you give yourself this score?

_____

_____

Based on your current score, look for areas of improvement in your life. Perhaps you can start seeing hardships as opportunities for improvement rather than something that is holding you back. Or perhaps you can speak more kindly—you may not always be able to control your thoughts but you can control what comes out of your mouth. Set a good example for yourself and your mindset will catch up. We may not be able to attain a "10" every waking moment, but you can certainly strive to jump from a six to a seven or from a seven to an eight if you are willing to make some daily mental adjustments. When you make positivity a priority, you'll see your happiness increase alongside.

Sunny Samples

1. Carmen: "I would say an eight overall. I am not perfect and I have off days. Sometimes life gets to be too much and I get sad about things. I am afraid and anxious for the future and I worry about money and school. In spite of this, I am still an eight because I am healthy, I have a wonderful family, great friends, an amazing boyfriend, a roof over my head, a car that runs, and I have a job."

2. James: "I'm at a nine. I don't think anyone can be a full 10, because bad things are bound to happen regardless of who you are. However, I think that the bad just makes you realize how good the 'good' actually is. I'm generally as happy as I can be."

3. Kianna: "If I had to pick an average, I'd say seven or eight. Most days nothing too exciting happens: work, school, eat, sleep, etc. But I'm still happy about being able to live my life. And then I get to have days where I do something exciting, like go on a hike with my family, or spend a day playing soccer and taking pictures. Even on a mundane day, it's finding happiness in the little things that makes life so important."

4. Addison: "I would say that on a day to day basis, my happiness level is about a seven. I have more good days than bad days, and I always feel thankful about one thing or another. But for some reason, I struggle with being content in my life, so this somewhat affects my happiness. I guess I feel that if something were different, or if I was skinnier, or if I had a boyfriend, then I would be happier."

5. Hallie: "My level of happiness on most days is an eight. I try to see the positive in all things, even a poor test grade or a flat tire. If I find myself in a situation that makes me unhappy, I do my best to get myself out of it or turn it around. Like recently, I've made the self-discovery that I don't actually feel happy around some of my 'best' friends. Instead of dwelling on the putdowns or negativity that they radiate, I try to surround myself with people that I think are beautiful; people who are happy."

6. Bryan: "At this moment in time I'm probably at a six. I have been on anti-depressants and just got off of them a month ago. I have had to deal with a lot of unfortunate events like break ups and let downs and it has really brought me down. I am slowly picking myself back up again."

7. Cody: "I give myself a 7.2 because I'm a college student still searching for what brings out happiness in myself and others. I feel like I should be giving back more to the community and I'm eager to start a career. On the flip side, I'm grateful for everything I've gotten to experience in my twenty years and I feel blessed to have a great education, a healthy relationship, and a giving family."

8.   Nina: "I'm currently at a three, but that is just because I am not in a very good mood. Lately I have been jumping from my average of eight to a low of three. I think it is just because I feel alone."

9.   Mia: "I'm at an 8; I usually don't let things or people bother me too much. I rarely get angry and when I do, I've learned to let it go quickly. Little things like someone saying 'hi' to me or seeing a hummingbird in my front yard can easily make me happy again.

10.   Tina: "I'm at a 10 right now. I used to be the type of person who was always waiting to be happy, you know the 'one day, once I do _____, then I'll be a happy kind of person.' I never realized how much I had to be grateful for and how happy I could be throughout life. Now I continually look for all the reasons I have to be happy, no matter how challenging life can become. As I learn to count my blessings, I have realized that the hard times and the challenges are actually the biggest blessings I have in my life. I have learned that these experiences allow me to become a stronger, happier individual."

Happiness: A Choice or For the Chosen?

At some point; you have to wonder, is happiness a choice? Or is it by chance, by fate, by genetics? Is it an internal hormonal state or do we choose how we feel? For some people, the answer was instantaneous when I asked them—is happiness a choice?—of course! But if you question this statement—the idea that people can just "choose" to be happy—I don't blame you. I'm a little leery myself. I don't think it's humanly possible to sit yourself down and tell yourself, "Now listen, you're going to be happy *or else.*" But we can be *open* to happiness. When we allow ourselves to be vulnerable enough to experience happiness, that is when we make a conscious choice to be joyful.

Genetics do play a role in our level of happiness. Many people experience depression in their life, which can make happiness incredibly difficult. I have interacted with many people who have experienced depression and they have conveyed to me how incredibly hard it can be to feel happy, as much as they may want to. And while not everyone may be clinically depressed, we've all experienced bouts of the blues. It's a human experience that we've all shared and I think we can all agree, sometimes allowing yourself to feel down can actually *feel good* in a way. Letting yourself feel sad is much healthier than forcing yourself to be happy, or to look happy, when you don't want to.

That's what makes true happiness special; it is a free choice and it is natural. It is not fake and it is not an act—it's completely genuine. So yes, I believe that you can choose to open yourself to the possibility of happiness—but you cannot command happiness. That never works. In fact, I find that I often rebel against it when it's forced. Can you relate?

Sunny Samples

1. April: "Happiness is both a choice and a part of our destiny. We have to choose to not let the small things get us down, but at the same time, some people are armed with superior coping mechanisms. I had an older lady friend who claimed that she had never once had a bad day. When I asked her secret, she said, 'I always look at my blessings and I can't help but be happy.' It was her natural tendency to always look up instead of down. I am much more of a cynical person by nature, so I have a harder time making that choice. But when I do, I am never disappointed by the results."

2. Paul: "Happiness is a choice. I think that most things in life are within the grasp of the individual, and happiness is no different. Just like how we choose whether to put in the effort to study for a test or to call an old friend, we make the choice to be happy or unhappy as well."

3. Bethany: "Happiness is only partially a choice. I think some people just 'fake' happiness. People can smile and dance on the outside while inwardly carrying a dark, empty hole of sadness. True happiness should not be such an effort for the individual, but should be naturally evident when someone experiences the joys of life."

4. Carrie: "Happiness is a choice. I am a firm believer that people can choose the way they feel. For example, I chose to leave my California home

and go to Washington for school. This big step led me to a severe depressive state at first. I thought I made the biggest mistake of my life. I became very irritable, was barely eating, and I thought there was no one in my life. I was sleeping about three hours every night and shaking during the day because I was in a new place surrounded by no one I knew. However, at the end of the first quarter, I had a great group of friends and got involved in the school's swim club. In this struggle of finding happiness in Washington, I found out it was up to me. I could have stayed in the shadows and fallen deeper in my depressive state. But nothing can make you happy unless you put in the effort."

5. Scott: "Happiness is inherent. There's no doubt about it. If someone close to you dies, you can't 'choose' to be happy. You're going to continue to be unhappy, and likely depressed. It's naïve to say that it's a choice."

6. Heather: "There is always something to be grateful for no matter what your situation. Sure, it is okay to be sad sometimes--it's only human. It means you have a heart. But happiness is absolutely a choice. 100%. For some people, it's just an easier choice."

7. Eve: "As a cognitive science major, I'm well aware of the effect of hormones on our bodies and our emotions. In spite of this, I believe, to some extent, we can control our moods. It takes a lot of patience, practice, and motivation to remain positive and happy, but I don't think it's impossible."

8. Paula: "For people that do not have any sort of medical reason, happiness is a choice. There are so many beautiful things in this world all around us that we take for granted. We miss the opportunity for them to bring us happiness. I 'chose' happiness once I realized this after being ignorant for so long."

9. Taylor: "I think happiness is BOTH a choice as well as innate. We must push ourselves to see the best in every situation and every person...we must choose to love even those who are hard to like. However, coming from families, on both sides, who are extremely affected by depression, I know that some aspects of unhappiness are inherent. Some imbalances exist that completely block the necessary chemical reactions to feel happiness and to stop worrying. I have to take medications just to stay at equilibrium

between sadness and happiness...and without this I would be much more troubled and probably much darker in terms of my personality."

10. Mika: "I like to believe that happiness is intrinsic in all of us. Sometimes we just don't see it."

Sunny Suggestion

Decide what your stance on happiness is. The answer is not usually black and white so think back. Were there situations in your life when you had the opportunity to be happy and instead you responded to it by complaining or pouting? How can you look on the sunny side a little more often? There is often a silver lining if you are willing to look for it. Instead of sulking in a situation, seek out the sunshine even in your darkest days. You'll come out stronger.

Your Sunny Side: Is happiness a choice or only for the chosen?

_____

_____

When did you have the opportunity to be happy but instead reacted by complaining? Why did you do this?

_____

_____

When did you choose to be happy in your life, even though it may have been challenging? Were you glad you reacted this way?

_____

_____

Your Happiness Harvest

Confession: I love metaphors. They give life a little more color. One of my favorites is the concept of harvesting your happiness. In our life, we have to pay close attention to what thoughts we are planting and growing in our minds. We have to ask ourselves: Am I nurturing my family life? My relationship with my friends? My future? Am I pursuing my passions? Am I taking steps to be a little bit closer to that dream career? We have to keep rotating our fields and refining our goals to make sure our mental harvest is happy and healthy. We have to be wise about what we sow so that we can be happy with what we reap.

We may not always be in a bountiful season in our lives, but we can't give up on our potential. Even in a bad harvest, there is at least one good potato. The Irish survived and so can we! Studying happiness made me much more aware of what in my life makes me joyful, even when I'm going through a distressing time. Here's my **Sunny Side** that gets me through it all, even when I've felt flooded with problems.

My Crops of Happiness

1. **Dancing with my friends**: I love to be with people who just—*get you*. And if you can get how I dance—then we're really meant to be. Whether we're out salsa dancing or we're just bringing back the lawnmower and shoplifter throwbacks (middle school dance moves in case you're confused), dancing with my girls helps me get my happiness in high gear.

2. **Laughing with my parents**: My dad is a comedy king. I love Saturday mornings when we sit with our cereal and coffee, turning any hardships of the week into humor. I highly recommend you find someone in your life that is like this—someone who gives you a better workout listening to their jokes than being at the gym because they make you laugh so hard. I like to call these people "happiness holders" because they carry and pass on so much happiness to the people that surround them. Get a hold of one of these people today and you'll notice an immediate difference in your attitude.

3. **Going to Disneyland**: It's only natural that I would frequent "the happiest place on Earth." I love visiting this sunny spot in California because it brings back some of my best childhood memories, especially dancing with my dad in a Disneyland parade (he danced with Tiger, I danced with Pooh). It's always a guaranteed happy day and I'll never tire of that Disney magic.

4. **Cuddling with my cat**: I really am becoming a cat lady. My pet brings me so much joy whenever he graces me with his presence. I could spend the whole day with him and feel perfectly content. Such a true companion.

5. **Driving in my car**: It's my me-time—which is something I think we should all carve out for ourselves. I can sing as loud (and as off-key) as I like, especially when "Don't Stop Believin'" comes on the radio—how can I resist?

6. **Baking**: I have to make the Cook family proud! Too bad I'm about one of the least talented cooks I know. Who put egg whites instead of egg yolks in the crème brulee recipe? Oh right, that was me. Oh well, it's all about fun when you're in the kitchen and I'm a top chef when it comes to that.

7. **Trying new things**: It's not necessarily in my nature to break out of my comfort zone but it's an invigorating feeling when I do. Whether it's trying a new hike or a new food, I always feel happy when I've had the guts to just go for it, whether or not I actually liked what I tried.

8. **Visiting the zoo:** If I lived another life, I think I would be a zoologist. Animals absolutely fascinate me and I could spend days at the zoo just watching animals play and interact. Whether it's gibbons or penguins, I'm guaranteed to smile.

9. **Going out to dinner**: More than eating delicious food, I love to have good conversations over a meal. Whether it's being adventurous and trying a new dish or hanging out at my favorite dining hideaway, I'm always happy when there's something scrumptious on my plate and I have someone to share it with.

10. **Writing:** I love how it is exhilarating yet soothing at the same time. Writing is like food for my soul; it comforts me. No matter how hectic

life gets or where I may be, I know that once I settle down I can get in touch with my spirit. I like seeing my thoughts come alive on paper.

So there you have it, ten things that make me happy. I could list many more, and I know you can as well, but these are some of my favorites. Here's how some of you are harvesting your own happiness.

Sunny Samples

1. Clarissa: "I think when most people imagine what would make them happy, they think of big, unrealistic events, like winning the lottery, but I don't see any reason why the accumulation of little joys in life can't add up to overall happiness. As far as I'm concerned, any day that involves frozen yogurt is a happy day."

2. Jessie: "Love brings me the most happiness. Love is the answer. Without it, the world would be a dull and lonely place."

3. Beth: "I am most happy when I feel that I am doing something that has purpose and meaning. I thoroughly enjoy knowing that God is on my side, supporting and blessing my endeavors. Pleasing God makes me the happiest."

4. Paige: "The things that give me pure happiness are animals. There is something so naive and innocent about the way they love humans. I wish we could love each other like that sometimes...to be so loyal, unquestioning, and unconditional. Animals may not be the most intellectual company but hands down all animals can make me laugh or intrigue me within minutes of seeing them."

5. Zach: "Making other people happy. When I can be the source of another person's good day, or even just a good moment, that's what truly makes me feel happy."

6. Jamie: "Honestly, as sappy as it sounds, the main source of my happiness is my boyfriend who turned *everything* around in my life. He supports me and makes me feel like everything, no matter what, will be okay. He exponentially increases my happiness and helps cut back the gloom."

7. Leslie: "I would have to say that music brings me the most happiness in my life. Whether it's playing or listening to it, I often cry because of the pure happiness music brings to me!"

8. Jared: "My friends are awesome and they are a huge part of my happiness. We are big nerds and we have epic adventures together. We depend on each other in a very literal sense and they are my new family. I have never had relationships as powerful and inspiring as these, and they make me the happiest person in the world."

9. Kimber: "Friends come and go but my family is a constant group of people who want nothing more than to see us smile. As my dad always says to me, 'Your happiness is my happiness.'"

Sunny Suggestion

I encourage you to write down 10 things that make you happy—both the big and the small. It may be something like baking in the kitchen with your best friend or roller-skating along the beach. If you're feeling stumped, list anything that makes you smile, laugh, or lose track of time. Better yet, don't let your list stop at 10. Write as many things that you can think of. And then, don't let it collect dust. Check back on your list frequently and add to it as you discover more of life's little joys. When you write your list be sure to elaborate so you can understand just why these activities make you so happy. Grow your list, harvest your happiness.

1. _____

2. _____

3. _____

4. _____

5. _____

6. _____

7. _____

8. _____

9. _____

10. _____

The Perfect Present

I love studying happiness because it is so applicable to everyday life. We all want to know the secrets of how to find it, how to keep it, and how to give it. Like eating or sleeping, we all want happiness to be a part of our routine. Happiness is meant for everyone at every age, and for every race, creed, and religion. Everyone can have happiness. From a newborn to a ninety-year-old, from a teenage girl to a mom with toddlers, from a student in Hong Kong to a teacher in Germany, there are no borders or boundaries to happiness. You deserve it, I deserve it. It is not a right (as we do not receive it automatically), but it is a privilege that we can try to access as much as we can. Like money, some may have more of it than others but everyone gets a payday at some point—it just depends how much you want to work for it. People who actively pursue an enriched life are much more likely to experience the richness of happiness than the people who wait for it to land on their doorstep.

But we can't just consider our own happiness. Our peers, our parents, and our future generations deserve happiness just as much as we do. The greatest gift we can offer the people in our lives is the gift of happiness. It may come in small doses, like a hug or a thoughtful message or it may come in a massive manner—like adopting a child or helping build a home for someone. But may these gifts of happiness come nonetheless—and may we be generous in offering them.

We all have so much to give with what we've been given. We may not live in mansions and we may not own a pair of Louboutin shoes, but we all have *something*. It may not be much in the "world's eyes", but it is something valuable in someone else's eyes—someone who needs help. The best gift we can give to those in need is to support them with a happy heart. Joy is too good to keep to ourselves—we need to share it. Without happiness, all the riches in the world would be meaningless.

Sunny Suggestions

Think of five ways you can give the gift of happiness to someone close to you and five ways you can give happiness to a stranger. Perhaps you can bring your mom a cup of hot tea or you can write your grandpa a letter recalling your favorite childhood memories with him. Or perhaps you can volunteer in your community at a local tutoring center to help a first grader learn how to read. Here are a few of my ideas to get you started but the opportunities are truly endless.

Sharing Happiness with Family and Friends

1. Give someone a good hug—just because.
2. Call an elderly relative and chat about their day.
3. Treat a friend to coffee.
4. Write a note of appreciation to a co-worker.
5. Congratulate a sibling for getting into college by taking them to their favorite restaurant.

Sharing Happiness with Strangers

1. Make eye contact and sincerely smile at someone as you pass them on the street.
2. Yield your place in line to someone obviously in a hurry.
3. Leave an inspirational quote on your bus or train seat when you exit.
4. Greet a store cashier and ask about their day. Look them in the eyes.
5. Leave a positive comment on a website that you enjoy.

Your Sunny Side for Family and Friends: What are your ideas?

1. _____

2. _____

3. _____

4. _____

5. _____

Your Sunny Side for Strangers: What are your ideas?

1. _____

2. _____

3. _____

4. _____

5. _____

Finding More Happiness from Your Memories

One of the best ways to experience happiness is to look back on your fondest memories. These special moments in your life are a part of who you are and they contribute to who you will become. It's essential that you make time for these memories—look back at pictures, home videos, and talk about them—don't let it slowly fade away from your consciousness. We need to remember and reflect on the moments when we've been blessed by happiness so we can have more of those experiences in the future.

Since we're getting to know each other, here are some of my happiest memories:

1. **Dancing with my dad**: I loved to dance with him when I was four and I love to dance with him now. Whether we're swing dancing or waltzing across the ballroom floor, my dad is my best man—with the best pair of feet to match. When Frank Sinatra comes on, there's no stopping us!

2. **Winning Miss Teen California**: It's an amazing feeling to hear your name called in that split second. I'll never forget how they played "Dancing Queen" by ABBA. That was a moment of sheer surprise, excitement, and uncontainable happiness. The kind of joy where you can't even begin to control that big grin that stretches across your face.

3. **Laughing with my friends**: They've shown me how much fun life is. Meeting certain girls throughout my life, whether it was when I was a baby or in college, has been one of the greatest blessings I've ever been given. Friends bring you to the best times and they get you through the worst. Never let your good friends go.

4. **Falling in love for the first time**: I feel fortunate that I had that experience at the perfect time in my life. I'm not sad that it's over; instead, I'm grateful for the memories.

5. **Finding out I got into UCLA**: I'll never forget checking my email at six am and seeing the "congratulations" banner across the screen. That was one of the happiest moments of my life because little did I know at that time, it would lead to some of the happiest years of my life. It's often in those flash moments that something magical is about to happen.

Here were some of your favorite memories:

Sunny Samples

1. Tori: "Some of my happiest memories are the vacations with my family. Rather than spending money to buy a lot of presents, my family would go on cruises to places like the Caribbean and Mexico for Christmas. The

presents that would one day be thrown away were instead turned into family memories that will last me a lifetime."

2. Lily: "My most recent overwhelmingly happy moment was in New York. I purposely didn't finish my meal so that I could give it to one of the many homeless people on the streets of Manhattan. The man I gave my meal to simply said 'thank you very much,' but the graciousness in his eyes said so much more."

3. Brittney: "I love my memories of climbing Vernal Falls at Yosemite with my parents, bringing home my first dog, Talula, winning the playoff game my senior year, camping on the beach with my friends for my 16th birthday, and playing soccer with locals in Costa Rica."

4. Mary: "One of my happiest memories was when I was 14 years old, away at camp. My entire grammar school life (first grade-eighth grade) was very difficult. I was always bullied, picked on, and harassed. I felt like the ugly duckling and just assumed people didn't like me. When I went to camp, it was the first time in my life that I made dozens of friends who encouraged me. I remember a camp counselor complimenting my personality and my ability to sing. In grammar school I was looked upon as non-athletic but at camp I came in third place during the two-mile run. It was an eye-opener that there was nothing wrong with me: I was not ugly, I was not boring, and I was not non-athletic. For the first time I realized the problem was with the bullies and I had a lot to offer as a friend. Since then I always feel happier by making sure people feel accepted for who they are."

5. Lynn: "My happiest memories are often ones with my family. I remember catching my first fish with my dad, dance team sleepovers, driving to LA after school to see shows with my mom, holding hands with the orphans in Ghana as I walked them to school, singing in the Girl's State choir, chatting with my favorite Starbucks barista, and buying ice cream for the children behind me in line at Baskin Robbins."

Sunny Suggestion

Get out your photo albums or home videos and write down some of your favorite memories. Perhaps you can even take some of those favorite pictures and put them up on your wall to continually remind yourself of the fun experiences you've had with your favorite people. And while I don't think Facebook should consume all of your free time, it's a great idea to look back on your photo albums. Reminding yourself of your happy memories will carry on those positive feelings into the present.

Your Sunny Side: What are some of your favorite memories?

1. _____

2. _____

3. _____

4. _____

5. _____

6. _____

7. _____

8. _____

9. _____

10. _____

Get Your Glow Going

I like to end each chapter with a quote. This one's written by Denis Waitley, the author of *The Psychology of Winning*:

"Happiness cannot be traveled to, owned, earned, worn or consumed. Happiness is the spiritual experience of living every minute with love, grace, and gratitude."

How are you living your life? Is happiness a new purchase or a new friend? Is happiness a huge wallet of cash or a huge hug from one of your best friends? Happiness comes in small packages but it also comes in grand gestures of generosity and gratitude. For our happiness to last, we've got to get our priorities straight.

And because it's the first chapter, let's kick it off with just one more quote by one of the student writers.

"To me *ultimate happiness* is that special glimmer or glow that certain people have. The glow is so easily recognizable. We have all seen it in others and are able to quickly identify it because as humans, we are naturally drawn to such genuineness. That glow only comes from obtaining *ultimate happiness*."

Are you glowing wherever you go? Are you radiating an appreciation for life or are you sending out signs of insincerity? It's your choice. You cannot control how people perceive you, but you can control how you perceive yourself and your life situation. You can choose to bask in the brilliance of life or you can choose to let yourself grow cold. Surround yourself with people who light up your life and be a light to others. Be open to the possibility of happiness in your life. It's ready and waiting for you.

Helping Equates to Happiness

While young adults may be labeled as selfish, I adamantly believe that our generation is also the most *selfless*. We have more resources than ever with the expansive outreach of technology and social media and because of this, we have the opportunity to spread happiness wherever we go by networking and making use of our connections. As we are now communicating through worldwide outlets, there are so many more opportunities to help a child learn to read, give a playground a make-over, or provide a homeless person with a home cooked meal. Happiness has never been more accessible to so many people—if we use these resources in the *right* way.

One of the happiest parts of this research for me has been learning what selfless acts young adults are doing on a philanthropic level, not only locally but also nationally and internationally. I am amazed by the many contributions of this generation and I think we need to celebrate them. It's some of the best news we've gotten in a world that is all too consumed by the worst. It is all too often that we hear about teens who are trapped in gang violence, drugs, or a failed education system. Yes, these are all tragedies that we need to be aware of and do something about but we must also recognize what's right in this world, like the millions of young adults who are making a positive difference. If you are not already one of these people who are taking steps toward beneficial change, I hope this book will be the motivation to get you started.

Paying It Forward

You may feel alone in your attempts, but even one selfless person can make a huge difference. I like to live my life "paying it forward." Inspired by one of my favorite movies, *Pay It Forward*, a little boy named Trevor is inspired by his teacher to change the world. A big homework assignment, I know. Yet Trevor comes up with a simple and explosive equation called "Pay it Forward." (Hence the title of the film). It begins with one person—just one. That one person does three huge acts of kindness. They are acts that the receiver could not have done on their own--things like taking in a homeless man until he can find a job or rescuing someone before they purposefully jump off a bridge. Once they are able, those three recipients then become givers to their own three people, affecting nine more. The process goes on and on. Now I'm not suggesting you take in a homeless person or go stand on the Golden Gate Bridge waiting to rescue someone. But you can do little things--unexpected things--to pay it forward every day. Happiness is sure to ensue when you focus more on the happiness of the greater good rather than just yourself.

Put Your Passion in Its Place

With this concept of paying it forward in mind, I think it is essential that we all find a community service project that we genuinely care about. When we have a passion with a purpose, we can be so much more effective in our helping. Yes, you may get school credit for it or at first you may be doing it for a college application, but ultimately, the rewards of service are far beyond a line on a resume. When we find something that matters to us—that means more than just our self-interest—that is when true help and true happiness ignite.

Why do we all need to offer our help when we can? Because we've all got problems. For example, almost everyone has been affected by cancer in some way. Some of us know what it's like to be living in a paycheck-to-paycheck home. Some of us know what it's like to have a family member leave the country to fight for our freedom. Life is happening all around us, and like fragile flowers, we can all get beaten down by the rain and wind. But that doesn't mean you can't save a wilting blossom. We need to help each other stay strong. When you are willing and wanting to help others, you have the opportunity to be that ray of sunshine for someone when all their skies have been cloudy and gray. Or you can be that bit of fresh rain when a drought of despair has dried up all of their hope. You can be an example of hope, courage, and happiness.

We all have our roots that make us the flowers we are. Roots aren't always pretty. In fact, they can be pretty ugly. We've all got our own history of illnesses, losses, and hard times that can be buried deep in our soil. But these roots, while they may not be the most picturesque part of a flower, are what make us strong. They carry our dedication, our courage and our resilience as we grow into something beautiful for everyone to see. Not everyone has to know what lies beneath the surface—only you know that. But everyone sees what you become. So be proud of where you came from and let it shape you into something that everyone admires and wants in their own garden.

Giving back is one of the greatest ways to grow your happiness. **My Sunny Side** lies with the American Cancer Society. Every year I participate in Relay for Life where I have helped raise over $70,000. Because my grandma, aunt, and mom are all cancer survivors, this is a cause that I truly care about. Until there is a cure, I won't stop fighting and fundraising. While I could be angry and resentful of our family situation, including the fact that I have an 80% chance of getting breast cancer if I have the BRCA I and II genes, I just don't have time for negativity. It's a waste of energy and a misuse of my emotions. I only have time for positivity. I share this with you because I want you to know that I am right there in the heart of it with you. We all have our battles; we have to fight back wisely. Bitterness is never as effective of a strategy as hope and bravery are.

There's one "sunflower" that has shone brightly in my life and in so many other's. Dallas Woodburn, an author, philanthropist, and future professor of creative writing, has been one of my greatest mentors to not only me but to hundreds of other writers. She has planted so much happiness in the lives of many children. I want to share part of her interview so that you can see just how amazing she is:

SG: Please tell us about your project, Write On!, and how you got started.

DW: I started Write On! For Literacy in 2001 to encourage kids to discover confidence, joy, a means of self-expression, and connection through reading and writing. My website www.writeonbooks.org features writing contests, book reviews, fun writing prompts, and more.

SG: Please tell us about your experience teaching children to write and how this has added to the happiness of you and the children.

DW: Every year I teach a Summer Writing Camp in my hometown for kids ages 8 -18. The goal is for students to have fun while also learning how to improve central components of their writing through various writing exercises. Many students are initially intimidated about writing and are shy about sharing their work, but by the end of camp they are much more confident in not only their writing skills, but in all aspects of themselves. I look forward to Summer Writing Camp all year long!

I have found that often when students are more receptive to exploring the world through reading and writing, they become more passionate about learning as a whole. Throughout the year, I frequently volunteer at schools to teach writing activities to kids. This is one of the most fulfilling things to me. Whenever I am feeling discouraged or creatively drained, going to schools and speaking to students inevitably recharges my batteries and gets me excited about writing again. There's so much energy and enthusiasm--it's contagious!

SG: How do you think your book donations have added to the happiness of the children who receive these books?

DW: After volunteering as a reading tutor for elementary school students, I was shocked to find that all of the books they had were tattered and torn--sometimes pages were even ripped out. So I began holding an annual Holiday Book Drive to collect new books for underprivileged kids. Our motto is: 'Toys are broken and clothing is outgrown, but the magic of books lasts a lifetime.' Unlike a new toy that breaks or grows boring, a book can be read again and again. A book can be a comfort during a hard time. A book can inspire you to positive action and can stick with you the rest of your life. Since we've started eight years ago, we've donated more than 11,000 books.

I have been told that, for many of the young recipients, these books are the only Christmas presents they receive. Furthermore, the books we collect and donate are often the first books these kids have ever owned. Libraries are wonderful resources, but it is different to have a new book for your very own, a book you can keep—you can write in the margins, dog-ear the pages, and take it with you everywhere. We do not only give books to disadvantaged youth—we give them hope, and the knowledge that someone cares about them. We help foster within them an ownership over reading—and, in turn, a sense of empowerment over their education and their life as a whole. When critics say that kids today don't care about books, that they only care about video games, computers, and TV, I challenge them to donate a box of books to their local Boys & Girls Club and see if they walk away with the same cynicism. Books are irreplaceable. When we walk in with the donated books, the kids swarm the boxes of books as if they were filled with candy. All year, I look forward to seeing the kids' excited smiles when they receive new books they can keep.

Isn't Dallas amazing? When you take your passion and put it to good use, the possibilities are endless. Throughout my research, I put an emphasis on discovering what young adults are doing to make a difference. I wanted to know where you're putting your energy, your healing, and your hope in the world. In the process, I learned that there is no place that has been left untouched by your helping hands.

Sunny Samples

1. Heather: "Recently, I traveled to Nepal, one of the ten poorest countries in the world, to volunteer in orphanages and schools. This has totally changed my perspective on gratitude. The people of Nepal,

especially the children, are so open, honest and resourceful. The poverty there is astounding, and the main source is a lack of stable infrastructure and government. Nepali people have a very difficult time understanding that their country is beautiful because they are surrounded by so much hardship. On our last day, it was so gratifying to give the teachers school supplies because all they had was a whiteboard and a clock. What we gave wasn't much at all by American standards-- just some paper, markers, and posters--but the teachers were so overwhelmed. When we tried to say that it wasn't much, one teacher responded by saying, 'Yes, but it's a lot for me.'

In Nepal, we were constantly explaining that we weren't rich Americans; we were in the low- end of middle class. But to the Nepali people, we are extremely wealthy. The things I am grateful for changed from my service there. I realized that I am truly wealthy, and that so many children have not had the stable childhood I have been blessed with. I am happy every day for all of my privileges, but even happier that I had the chance to work with what I believe to be the most wonderful culture in the world."

2.   Hunter: "I've done lots of volunteering with Project Understanding, passing out food for the poor and homeless. It's sometimes very hard to see the desperate situations some people are in but I find it extremely gratifying to help and interact directly with these people."

3.   Angela: "I go to local animal shelters and spend time with the ugliest animals there (especially the ones would probably never be adopted). It makes me feel good to give an animal attention who longs to get out of a cage. I have a huge heart for animals."

4.   Ray: I feel most happy when I do small random acts of kindness from saying 'hi' and smiling at someone on the street that looks sad to helping an elderly person in the grocery store. It makes people feel really good when someone goes out of their way to help them with no expectation of anything in return."

5.   Emily: "It's hard not to feel good when you're making other people feel good."

❀   ❀   ❀

There's another individual, Greg Woodburn (yes, his sister is Dallas—an impressive family I know!) that I particularly want to highlight for his amazing accomplishments. He is proof that a great idea and an even greater motivation can lead to truly inspirational results.

SG: What is the basis of your organization, Give Running?

GW: Give Running shares a love for running, as well as the many other benefits and opportunities running provides. Our organization collects, cleans and donates new and used running and athletic shoes to disadvantaged youth in third world countries and local inner-city communities. (In the process, Give Running educates youth about the sport of running). Together, we can make a world of difference to deserving youth from Los Angeles to Haiti to as far away as Africa by giving them a chance to lace 'em up and to never stop running!

SG: How happy did you feel when you donated the shoes to the people in Africa?

GW: Even though I had played giving out the shoes over and over in my mind, nothing could prepare me for the actual experience. The first pair of shoes we gave to the village chief, and I remember as I helped put on his socks and shoes my hands were visibly shaking with excitement, adrenaline, and joy. The happiness of giving in Sikoro, Mali saturates me with more than just my time there— it continues to bring me happiness and pride as I look back on the memory. The experience continues as those men, women, and children are hopefully wearing their shoes right now.

SG: What has been the biggest challenge of the project and how has this affected your happiness? How did you overcome it?

GW: I think Give Running's greatest blessing has also been its greatest challenge. It's been the overwhelming support from people who have learned about our cause and want to become involved. Indeed, Give

Running has quickly grown to include shoe donation drives and events across the country and around the world, which have inspired me but also caused logistical challenges and trial-by-fire in some cases. The stress of problem solving can definitely affect my happiness, but keeping things in perspective helps me maintain peace of mind.

SG: How did the children display their happiness upon receiving the shoes?

GW: As in most cases, the happiness and magic of the moment was mostly conveyed through their eyes. The children's eyes had become playful and bright since we had arrived, and both their hosting of us, and our giving to them filled us all with the reciprocal joy of helping.

Sunny Suggestion

What philanthropies inspire you? If you're not feeling drawn to a particular organization, can you see yourself starting up your own project? No idea is too big or too small when the end goal is to help someone. You can be the one to start up your dream or you can be part of a dream that's already coming true, like charities such as Habitat for Humanity or the American Red Cross—both of which already have thousands of volunteers. What form of service will bring you and others the most happiness?

Your Sunny Side: What cause do you want to help with and how will you do this?

_____

_____

_____

_____

The Five Daily Gratitudes

There's one word that keeps returning when it comes to giving back: *gratitude*. Gratitude is a concept that I try to integrate into my life on a daily basis and I hope you will as well after reading this book—if you're not already. It is the ultimate secret to happiness that many of us underutilize. The good news is that being consciously aware of your feelings of gratitude will soon become second nature if you are willing to make the effort. When you integrate an attitude of gratitude into your life as a mindset rather than an occasional thought, it could be the key that unlocks the door to your happiness.

For better or for worse, we humans are very adaptive creatures. Think about it. One minute, we walk into a room with the delicious smell of chocolate chip cookies wafting through the kitchen and five minutes later, you can't tell the difference if it was cookies or cauliflower cooking. The same applies to gratitude. If we don't actively focus and recognize it in our lives, its presence becomes quickly unnoticeable. The little butterfly on the windowsill shifts from a beautiful gift of nature to just another insect flying around. The embrace of a good friend becomes another casual greeting. A special "I love you" becomes another common tagline. We have to be careful. It's easy to be nonchalant but; in actuality, we have to take notice and actively pursue gratitude on a daily basis.

That's why I developed **The Five Daily Gratitudes**. What is it? Well, every night, before you go to bed (or let's be realistic, any time of the day that you can take a few minutes for yourself), actively focus on five things that made you grateful that day. It may be something as simple as a flower you spotted on your way to class or it may be something more monumental—like your wonderful relationship with your mom. The beauty of The Five Daily Gratitudes is that it creates a moment for you to celebrate your gratitude when before you may have missed it. You'll start noticing joys in your life that previously went unnoticed and you'll have a deeper appreciation for the aspects of your life that you were already thankful for.

I've been writing my Five Daily Gratitudes for over a year now and because of it, I'm a noticeably happier person. I celebrate so much more of the world now. I look for things to be grateful for, whereas before, giving thanks was a nice afterthought while I chowed down on turkey every Thanksgiving. Now, gratitude has become a daily holiday, not just a once-a-year celebration of gluttony and giblets. (Not sure I'm grateful for that part anyway.)

So here are a few of my Five Daily Gratitudes. They may seem a bit random but on the day I wrote them, they were relevant. Bonus: when you look back on those days, you'll be able to remember the details that much better. Those memories of happiness can live on past the initial moment. When I write mine, I always try to give a little Sunny Girl gusto—I think it's more fun when you give your list your own personal flavor.

1. **Blisters**: Because those brand new shoes were too cute not to wear on my first day of work. But I'll take the blisters any day because it means I have a job that I love. Still, I won't be wearing those shoes for a while!

2. **Writing**: I finally found my passion. Some people have to run every day, my fingers have to type every day.

3. **"Walking on Sunshine"**: When that song plays on the radio, all the other cars on the road better watch out because my theme song just came on.

4. **Giving presents**: I love finding great gifts for special people in my life. Especially when it's unplanned—there's nothing better than stumbling, and then pouncing, on that perfect present.

5. **Asking questions**: It doesn't always come naturally to me when I'm in a classroom setting but I usually feel more stupid when I don't ask my "stupid" question to begin with, which probably wasn't really stupid at all. Don't be afraid to find out what everyone else is wishing they had the courage to ask about.

A year from now, I guarantee I will remember my days all the better because I have taken the time to savor some of the special moments. I am grateful for something new every single day and that gratitude carries on throughout the year. Even if you have to look under every nook and cranny for the smallest niche of a nicety, it's always worth it. You'll see your happiness grow on a daily basis if you start recognizing how much you really have to be thankful for in your life.

Sunny Suggestion

I encourage you to start making this a part of your daily routine. You can even get yourself a journal that can be just for your Five Daily Gratitudes. You'll quickly see how easy and time efficient this practice is while giving you a tremendous happiness boost—it's especially great when you've had a tough day. If you really want to get the most out of this exercise, I recommend explaining the significance of each of the five—don't just *list* your choices. You'll reflect more on the moments when you go into detail. Also, when you look back, you'll have a better understanding for why you were thankful that day. There's no better time to start than today:

Your Sunny Side: Five Daily Gratitudes

1. _____

2. _____

3. _____

4. _____

5. _____

Giving Back Gratitude

It's great to keep a record of your Five Daily Gratitudes, but more than just making a note of it for yourself, it's even better to give your gratitude back to others. We need to show our appreciation otherwise it is merely *self-gratification*. So, how do you thank others?

Your Sunny Side: How do you currently express gratitude to others?

_____

_____

Perhaps you give gifts or write thank you notes. Maybe you give a hug or you invite a special person to spend more time with you. Or you might be someone who feels too shy or too lazy to express gratitude. Well, no matter where you're at, it's time for a shake-up. There's always room for improvement and whether it comes naturally to you or not, I have faith that you can become an excellent expresser of gratitude. If there's anything to perfect in life, it's this! You'll quickly see that when you pass on your appreciation to others, not only will you bring them joy, that joy will be much more profound on a personal level for you. Here are some start-up ideas for getting your gratitude in high gear.

Sunny Samples

1.   Kaitlin: "I express my gratitude openly and often. Whether it's just a smile or a thank you note, I always feel my spirits lifted when I seal the envelope. I know it will brighten someone's day, even on the smallest level, because whenever I receive others thanks I feel like a queen! Expressing gratitude is such an easy way to get so much more out of life. I find that when I express gratitude, I make more friends, meet more people, and touch more lives."

2.   Anne: "I always write thank you notes. And on top of that if I get something really special I will call the person. Also, to show my appreciation towards my parents, I help out around the house. And I go all out on their birthdays, Mother's Day, Father's Day, and other holidays. I make sure to emphasize why they deserve such great gifts because they mean so much to me."

3.   Kathryn does this: "I love to surprise people with thoughtful gifts or letters to let them know I appreciate them. I know it feels good to have

someone recognize your hard work, so, in turn, I compliment others to make them feel special."

Here are some of my tried and true tips that I have collected over the years. These Sunny Suggestions are sure to be a win-win for you and the people you are thanking.

Sunny Suggestions

1.   Write a thank you note. Sending a *handwritten* thank you note is one of the best ways to convey your gratitude. If someone went out of their way for you, then you can reciprocate by sending a nice note. It takes five minutes yet it is a timeless tradition that expresses your thoughtfulness, politeness, and appreciation. And no, I hate to break it to you, email or Facebook just doesn't cut it. Call this a pitch to keep Hallmark in business, but they've been around this past century for a reason. I'm not saying that you have to buy the elaborate stationary with glitter and rhinestones but whether it's Papyrus, the drug store, or it's homemade, sending a card can make all the difference. And in case you tend to be a master procrastinator, it's better to strike when the iron is hot. General etiquette says you should send a thank you note within seven days. But if you catch yourself at the seven-day mark and on, it's still "better late, than never!" And then my grandma loves to add: "But never late is better."

2.   Send a little, personalized gift. Get that special someone something that symbolizes their personality or a special part of your relationship with them. You don't have to get something elaborate (in fact that could make them feel guilty and indebted). Be smart but savvy about your spending choices when it comes to gifts. Ultimately, the key is just to get something small but special—enough to say that you were thinking of them.

3.   Let's get physical. Not Olivia Newton-John style. A simple hug works wonders. And if you don't think a hug is appropriate, then don't do it. There's nothing more awkward than the half-hug, half-handshake number. So if your potential hugger isn't the cuddly teddy bear type, or the occasion doesn't warrant it, then a handshake is always acceptable to express your gratitude.

4. Return the favor. If someone invites you to be their guest, it's important that you eventually return the favor. No one likes a mooch. Be the one to offer a favor or an invitation, don't be the one who is only accepting them. I don't recommend keeping a tally on who does what when it comes to hosting (in fact this will be a huge happiness hang-up), but people do subconsciously notice if you are the one who is always a gracious host or if you're the one who is always just showing up and reaping the benefits of other people's hard work. You've got to put in your time so that other people can have a good time. Ultimately everyone will be happier when it's equal—not to mention, hosting can be just as much, if not more fun, than being a guest!

Your Sunny Side: What can you do to improve the ways you are expressing gratitude?

_____

_____

_____

What are three new strategies you can try for showing your appreciation?

1. _____

2. _____

3. _____

5. **Say it in person.** If you're at a party or an event where the host has worked hard to prepare, I recommend taking the following three steps:

   • Greet your host and thank them for inviting you. This should be one of the first things you do when you arrive—don't sit back in the shadows. Added points: offering to help and bringing a small gift—no matter what the occasion.

- Compliment something specific. Maybe you love the cupcakes. Or you love the party favors. Find a unique effort that the host made to make the event extra special and make note of that. Be a stand out guest by noticing what stands out in the first place.

- Thank your host before you leave. Greetings and goodbyes are your opportunities to make the party planner feel appreciated. Don't leave an event without conveying how glad you were that you could be there. Even if it wasn't the best party you've ever been to, letting the host know that you had a good time will make him or her feel like their effort was worth their while. A happy host is one that knows that they have happy guests.

Get in the Game of Giving Back

You don't have to start your own writing summer camp or donate shoes to Africa (like the Woodburn family did), but I do hope that after reading this chapter you'll be motivated to be a source of hope rather than stand in the shadows. Savor this time in your life when you are able bodied and mentally capable to make as much of a difference as you desire. We have so much potential—we can't let it spoil. My dad always reminds me how important it is to use my talents to help others. He uses Edmund Burke's quote to share this message:

"All that is necessary for evil to triumph is for good men to stand by and do nothing."

If we stand by the sidelines, watching people get diagnosed, suffer, and die of diseases, we are only perpetuating the pain of this world. If we allow our troubled youth to just fester on the streets instead of helping them with their education and career opportunities, we are allowing our future to take a turn for the worst. We are ultimately promoting unhappiness when we turn the other cheek. Instead, we need to get in the game of giving back. We need to spread happiness by emphasizing health, educating everyone, and encouraging others to give their time and money to the causes they care about.

I don't mean to sound drastic, but we are in dire times, and more than ever, our help and our happiness are desperately needed. This is no time to be a benchwarmer. Those in our generation have to be star players; people are counting on us to make a touchdown. Everyone is watching to see what we will do—will we come up with a strategy, will we use our teammates effectively, and will we make that winning play? Or conversely, will we buckle our knees and get attacked by the other team? I have a strong belief that we can be the help that our local communities, country, and world needs if we let our happiness fuel our motivation. Nothing is impossible with a positive attitude and a passion to work hard. I am convinced that our generation has just that—we just need to work together so that we can all get in the game of giving back.

Some of us are given so much, and some of us are given so little. But with the means we *do* have, we can all make our own difference. It may not be much, but it may just be enough to change a person's life for the better. We have to mean something to each other and we have to mean something to this world. By "meaning," I do not mean fame or recognition. I mean *inspiration*. We all need to be an inspiration in our own way—we need to inspire each other to be better and happier people who love one another and strive for continual improvement. We should always give back, no matter how much we have been given. Only then can we start to lead happier lives. Because when we give back selflessly, we can know in our hearts that our happiness is not solely for ourselves, rather, it is so that other people can lead happier lives as well. Happiness is best when it's shared.

A Happy Heart = A Healthy Heart

Hopefully you are itching to save the world after the last chapter but, before you run out the door, make note: it's so much harder to make others happy if you're not happy. And if you're not healthy, happiness is going to be even harder to come by. So let's cover our bases.

Happiness and food have a very interesting relationship in America. We often use food as a reward system rather than as a biological resource for survival. You've heard the saying, "Some live to eat. Others eat to live." I think there's a balance. It's hard to be happy if you are always depriving yourself of some of the foods you enjoy (because let's be honest—food can make us happy!) but at the same time, you won't be happy if food is your only source of joy.

Second to the word "happiness" in this book, you'll hear me say "balance." You might feel momentarily happy when you take a bite into that chocolate glazed donut (can mine have the rainbow sprinkles, please?) but I don't think you can be truly happy if you're not living a healthy, *balanced* lifestyle. Sure, we all need our little splurge every now and then— key lime pie is my personal favorite—but overall, it is essential that we take care of our physical heart if we want to have a happy heart as well.

You might not realize what a good thing you have until it's gone. It's so easy to take our health for granted. *So easy.* But the second we feel that lump in our throat coming on (ugh, the common cold) or that pain in

45

our knee on our routine jog—we realize instantaneously—the health of our bodies can make or break our bliss. Or what about if you get in a car accident and can no longer walk? Having legs, having eyes, and having a fully functioning brain can all seem like something we deserve but we can quickly learn that nothing is ours to keep forever. Your health affects your life in everything you do—including your happiness.

This was one of the most enlightening chapters to research because this topic hits so close to home for everyone. I wanted to find out how people perceived their body image and how healthy they actually felt. I asked questions regarding diet, exercise, and sleep. Many people reported feeling great about their health and body image—lucky them. But many people were not so comfortable to share. The truth is, so many young adults are in the heart of their health hardships. I'm just leaving behind some health issues myself, and I can tell you, we are dealing with a lot when it comes to loving or hating our love handles. Our health and body image are some of the most private battles—as much as the public popularizes them.

My goal with this chapter is that you will be able to find some comfort in knowing that many people feel exactly the way you do, whether you feel secure in your stature or you're fighting a war with the mirror every day. I hope that you will be able to overcome whatever health and weight issues you have so that you can finally have a fair shot at happiness because quite frankly, the battle with the bulge along with the battle with boniness is one of our biggest threats to happiness. Many of us obsess over our appearance so much that our happiness doesn't even stand a chance. Part of the reason why I'm writing this book is so that you can have that chance once again because that is something you deserve. So let's start. No one is going to read this but you so I encourage you to really be honest with yourself.

Your Sunny Side: How do you feel about your physical appearance?

How do you feel about your overall health, regardless of how you look in the mirror?

_____

_____

_____

Eating Away at Our Joy

Even though anorexia is indeed becoming a worldwide problem, America's young women especially struggle with this disorder. I took a fantastic course as a freshman in college about the female body image and how it affects our happiness. As someone who had been obsessively on a diet for three years, this course changed my life. Reading Naomi Wolf's *The Beauty Myth* was a huge wake-up call for me. She discusses how work, culture, religion, hunger, and violence all contribute to anorexia by being some of the biggest killers among teenage girls.

I was by no means anorexic. And Lord knows I could never be a bulimic with my phobia of vomiting (I wish I was kidding but it's a legitimate fear of mine). But I was obsessed with food. I had to meticulously write down everything I ate. I went to bed wondering what I would get to eat the next morning and I went through the day, every day, calculating my calories. Eventually I came to realize I would never be happy counting down the hours till my next meal, weighing myself three times a day, or pulling out that damn measuring scale to tell the difference between two ounces of cheese versus three ounces of cheese. Are you serious? Unfortunately, at that point in my life, I was. It was mentally, physically, and emotionally draining. And I never actually lost any weight; in fact I gained weight.

In my opinion, what I went through is an eating disorder—I don't think two labels (anorexia nervosa and bulimia) cut it considering how individual eating disorders are on a broad spectrum. When you think about food more than you think about your friends, your family, your boyfriend or girlfriend, your academics, and your passions in life—it's an eating disorder. How could I let a bowl of brown rice take over my life? It doesn't hug, it's sure not cute, and it certainly doesn't make me happy like a good movie or a night with friends. It was time to break up my love affair with food.

That's why I have to talk about this and be honest about what I went through. Although our health and body image are only part of our overall identity, they can play a major role in our self-esteem and overall happiness. When we let something petty, like food, consume our lives, how can we allow any room for real happiness? Maybe we think happiness is a smaller dress size, and maybe it is, I won't deny that, but happiness won't come from obsessing about food. It comes from taking good care of your body. It is by loving yourself enough that you want to take good care of yourself, just not obsessive, calorie-by-calorie care.

Maybe you feel yourself starting to slip into this struggle or maybe this is a battle that you've been in for years. No matter where you are in this battle, we all need to ask ourselves every now and then, is food eating away at my happiness? You'll know the answer—I knew it all along, for quite a long while, I just didn't want to admit it to myself. And just so you know, this isn't just a "girl thing" either—men are increasingly being diagnosed with eating disorders as well. So for those of you that are in that place, I can relate. I don't know how you may feel specifically but I'll tell you how I felt—*trapped*. If I went a day without writing down what I ate, all was lost. I certainly wasn't happy at the time, although I believed the end goal would lead to happiness. It didn't.

I learned something though, not all was lost, not in the least. It may take some time, but hope and happiness are always possible. Once I was ready to let go of the "control" that I thought I had (which was actually a total loss of control), I realized that my obsession weighed more than any actual pounds did. So how did I do it? I gave myself time. I took baby steps. I slowly stopped writing down every bite I took. I stopped obsessively weighing myself every morning. I read books like *The Beauty Myth* and *Survival of the Prettiest*, by Nancy Etcoff. These were books that taught me I was not alone and I didn't have to live feeling like I was imprisoned by food. I discovered that I am a beautiful girl no matter what that number on the scale is and I deserve to be happy. I set myself free. It's been one of the best choices I've ever made.

Here's what other people had to say about their self-image and health.

Sunny Samples

1. Emma: "Many teenage girls have self-esteem issues. I have suffered from anorexia and have had to deal with critical body image issues on a daily basis. I am still in the process of overcoming my anorexia, though it may not look like I ever had it. It is a disease that will never go away, but I find ways to cope. Body image is a key to my happiness. I hate looking in the mirror every day. I obsess over it and I pick out every little detail of what I do not like about myself. I come from a very supportive family, but my mother has always been critical of me and that has affected the way I see myself. Nevertheless, we need to feel beautiful inside and out. We need to come to terms with the fact that we were given this body for a reason and that we should respect ourselves."

2. Brian: "I think my body image is a large factor in my happiness. If I worried a lot about the way others see me, my happiness would suffer. However, I have learned to accept my flaws and see myself as God's creation, rather than judge myself based on socially-inflicted standards, and thus, I do not allow bodily fluctuations to interfere with my happiness."

3. Katie: "As a female living in the US, the media shoves living skeletons down our throats and we learn that's what it is to be beautiful. I think of women like Betty Page and Marilyn Monroe who were beauty icons of their time because of their genuine female figure, but now they would be considered plus size and 'fat.' I try to keep a positive body image because I know my weight for my height is where it should be and my Body Mass Index (BMI) is normal but it's still difficult in the kind of society we live in today. It is very sad and could make even the happiest woman self-conscious and unhappy."

Here are some tips that can help enable you to live your healthiest and happiest life.

Sunny Suggestion

1. Be aware of your "self-talk." I'm fat. I'm too skinny. I'd be happy if I were taller, shorter, had curly hair, straight hair, a smaller nose, bigger muscles, longer legs. Do any of these statements sound familiar? Are you used to putting yourself down? Are you telling yourself lies? If so, you're not alone but it's time to embrace your curls, your curves, and your cut. Be proud of who you are!

Your Sunny Side: Do you put yourself down when it comes to your reflection in the mirror? If so, what do you nit-pick about?

_____

_____

What can you do to improve your self-image? How can you be kinder to yourself?

_____

_____

2. Start talking "nice" to yourself. Negative self-talk will rob you of happiness and sabotage your goals towards having a healthier body image. Write down ten things you love about yourself on post it notes and stick them around the house to remind yourself of how special you are.

Your Sunny Side: What are ten things you love about yourself?

1. _____

2. _____

3. _____

4. _____

5. _____

6. _____

7. _____

8. _____

9. _____

10. _____

Happy Hour

On the flip side of dieting, let's face it; feasting on good food can make us extremely happy. There's nothing like a delicious meal, especially when it's shared with people we care about. Many people commented on how happy food makes them, with particular mention to what happens when there is NO food. And I can tell you, after living with sorority girls, it is not a pretty picture when there is no food. A herd of grazing gazelles can become stampeding buffalo when there aren't enough mini pizzas or chicken nuggets to go around. There's no fight or flight—it's food or fight.

Food is a baseline for happiness. If our baseline biological and physiological needs are not being met, it's a surefire challenge to be psychologically happy. It's an incredibly basic concept but it's nonetheless fundamental to our happiness. And while it's important to treat ourselves every now and then, it is also essential that we fuel our bodies properly. If we let ourselves run on fumes, our happiness is going to break down by the side of the road. The choices that we make today establish habits and practices for the rest of our lives. A lot of you could relate:

Sunny Samples

1. Julie: "Food has a lot to do with my happiness. If I don't have one delicious meal in a day, then I'm not totally happy or satisfied. Food can put me in a good mood or a bad mood depending on if I liked it or if ate too much of it."

2. Christi: "I absolutely LOVE food and it makes me very happy. I am happy when I am eating comfort food like peanut butter, ice cream, cheesecake—basically anything with tons of carbs and sugar. But that also makes me upset after I eat it because I know that stuff is bad for the body and will make me unhealthy and overweight. When I eat veggies, fruit, and whole grains I am happy because I know that what I am eating is good for me."

3. Justin: "I am a triathlete, and have always been heavily involved in sports, so most of the time I have a very large appetite. I enjoy eating natural, healthy foods as well as the occasional Cold Stone ice cream treat or a slice of Costco pizza. Mostly, I'd say that food has a very positive effect on my happiness...especially the right type and quantity of food at the right time!"

Sunny Suggestion

1. Unlearn patterns of emotional eating. Many children are given sweets as a way to stop their crying and many of them learn to link cookies with comfort. This brings up a curious question, "Does anyone take comfort in carrots and celery sticks?" Not really. What they're finding is that high-fat, high-sugar foods, like ice cream, may activate certain chemicals in the body that create a sense of contentment and fulfillment—something that carrots just can't do because of an evolutionary hardwiring. This almost addictive quality may actually make you reach for these foods again when you're feeling upset, even when you're grown up and "should know better." It's not easy to unlearn these patterns of emotional eating, but it is possible if you have the right mindset. It's about finding happiness in other forms. It's never smart to rely on a sundae as your only source for a potential smile.

Your Sunny Side: What can you do to change any emotional eating habits you have?

_____

_____

2.   **Consider this chart.** Which side are you on most of the time?

Physical Hunger	Versus	Emotional Hunger
Tends to come on gradually, can be postponed	VS	Feels sudden and urgent
Can be satisfied with a number of foods	VS	Causes very specific cravings
Once full, you're likely to stop eating	VS	You tend to eat more than you need
Doesn't cause feelings of guilt	VS	Afterwards, can cause guilt

3.   **Make your own healthy Happy Meal.** Maybe you've moved on from the plain cheeseburger and fries (of if you're like me, you still love a good burger and fries); but it's never too late to put a nutritious spin on the foods that you love. You can make small adjustments without having to drastically adjust your waistband. It's a win-win for happiness. You'll be happy that you're still eating the foods that you love but you'll also be happy that you won't be gaining pounds that you may not love. P.S. the toy, that is often included with the burger, is optional. But just in case, a girl toy please. (I always loved the mini Barbies).

Your Sunny Side: What are three ways you can improve your eating habits while not feeling deprived?

1. _____

2. _____

3. _____

Exercise Your Right to Feel Alright

It's true—exercise is one of the quickest ways to get happy because of the chemical reaction that takes place during and after a good workout. A recent study by the American College of Sports Medicine has shown that just one 30-minute exercise session can boost your mood and beat depression. Now there's a reason to hop on the treadmill. Or if you're like me, to get outside and play a game of tennis.

I'll be honest. I don't love working out—blessings to those of you who actually look forward to going to the gym. But there is one thing that I do love—happiness—and that is what gets me in gear. Both the physical endorphins and the emotional boost from accomplishing a goal always feel great. So even though it may be a daily challenge, if I can do it, then you can do it. Whether you can't wait to hop on your bike or you'd rather make bicycle movements between your bowl of ice cream and your mouth, exercise is a manageable goal where there is always room for improvement.

The first step is to stop seeing exercise as a death sentence or some kind of torture device—you don't have to push yourself until you're in pain. In fact, exercise can be extremely fun when we tailor it to our interests. It can be an escape, a reversion to our childhood memories, and for me--a chance to listen to my favorite music—all of which can make us incredibly happy in the process.

Sunny Samples

1.   Matt: "Exercise makes me happy because I know I am doing something that is good for my body. Also exercise makes me, and everyone else for that matter, happy because of the endorphins the brain releases as we exercise."

2.   Samantha: "I would prefer to be doing something active every day. Whether it's going to the gym, walking somewhere, dancing, swimming, or hiking; being active makes me happy because it's good for my body and my mind."

3.   Ashley: "Exercise serves as an outlet for me, but it's different for every person. Everyone has their 'outlet' and one of mine is the gym. If I had a bad day or I was upset about something, the gym is there to help me cool down by burning it off. It relieves my stress in every aspect of my life and without it, I would be a lot more tense."

4.   Daniel: "Exercising helped me burn calories and burn off stress from school and other aspects of my life. I would listen to music that would represent my anger or aggression at times and working out helped me center those emotions. It helps keep your heart healthy and is ultimately good for your entire body."

5.   Laura: "I feel refreshed after a good work out. I feel clean on the inside and the outside."

Sunny Suggestions

1.   **Add variety.** The elliptical machine starts to literally make me feel like a lab rat, growing a tail and whiskers if I spend another day on it. You've got to switch it up. Maybe you love the outdoors, or you love to be in the water—try out different activities on different days so that your routine stays dynamic rather than dry.

Your Sunny Side: What are three ways you can spice up your work out?

1. _____

2. _____

3. _____

2. Do what you've always loved. If you loved to play baseball as a kid, join a league for adults. You'll feel so much happier when you treat yourself to exercise that you enjoy rather than when you torment yourself to the same dull repetition. If you loved something in the past, you'll probably like it in the present. Dust off those ballet shoes or those soccer cleats—you're never too old to get back in the game.

Your Sunny Side: What are some of your favorite childhood activities that you can incorporate into your workouts now?

1. _____

2. _____

3. _____

3. Let yourself learn something new--even if you feel like a fool. Yes, I thought I could figure out how to bench press until I got stuck trying and had to roll the bar down my entire body because I wasn't strong enough to lift it back up (and mind you, it was the bar—and only the bar). But I learned my lesson—use a spotter who can pick up the whole darn thing when my little arms give out. The same thing applies to any activity—you've got to keep making attempts and practicing, even if there is potential for a blush-worthy moment. Don't be afraid to ask for help, but more importantly, don't be afraid to try new experiences. Life is too short to only have a short list of adventures.

Your Sunny Side: What are some new workouts that you can try—even though it may scare you at first?

1. _____

2. _____

3. _____

A Lesson From the Cat: The Value of Sleep

What would all of this healthy eating and exercising be without a good night's sleep? A zombie is still a zombie, even if it's eating green beans and doing squats. Don't numb your brain by not getting enough sleep at night. You may be thinking that it's ridiculous to emphasize the importance of sleep in a book about happiness, but seriously—are you happy when you're half awake? It may seem obvious but I want to take a moment to appreciate the power of rest—it can make or break your day. If you want your happiness to be a priority in your life, then rest is essential.

When we're not "all there," our happiness isn't either. Lack of sleep has also been linked to slowed responses, poor concentration, and emotional troubles, such as feelings of sadness and depression. We tend to complain more, feel more distracted, and just go through life in a brain fog. I personally hate June gloom in California—why create your own personal dreary season on a daily basis? Sleep is simply essential. It helps keep us physically healthy and emotionally happy by slowing our body's systems enough so that we can re-energize.

Sunny Samples

1. Trevor: "If I don't get a good night's sleep I'm usually in a crabby mood. But when I wake up nice and rested I feel like I can take on the world!"
2. Jacob: "I am very conscious of the amount of sleep that I get as a student-athlete. I have always valued sleep in order to avoid getting sick

or stressed in life. The more I sleep, the more refreshed, clear-headed, and happy I am."

3. Liz: "If I'm lucky, I get an average of five hours of sleep every night. Then I am able to go about my daily activities, but I feel exhausted doing so. Sleep can affect our moods, our appearance (which affects the way we view ourselves), and our demeanor. With a lack of sleep I tend to be in a worse mood and I don't usually want to go out and do things because I lack the energy. As long as I can remember, I have suffered from insomnia. Let me tell you, it is not easy to deal with. I lay awake each night worrying about falling asleep because I know that I will not want to wake up the next day. It affects the way I think in school. I tend to fall asleep during class and on top of that I have A.D.D., which makes it even worse. Getting 8-10 hours of sleep each night would improve my mood and help me to think more clearly. It would help me to be more alert and live a safer and healthier life."

Perhaps you experience this every night, like Liz, or it happens on the rare occasion. But you can only count so many sheep before you want to slaughter one out of aggravation. Whether you've got a nagging thought or you're just uncomfortable from a humid night, tossing and turning has got to be one of the most simple happiness stealers out there. And it has lasting effects that carry on through the next day.

It's essential that we do our best to relax and get a good night's rest. Of course, not every night will we be sleeping between satin sheets and waking up to a rose on our pillow (I have yet to experience even *one* of those nights—maybe I'll put a flower there myself one of these days), but we still need to give ourselves the gift of a good night's rest. Sleep is happiness in its most humble form. If you want a shot at happiness, here are some Sunny Suggestions to get you sleeping in no time.

Sunny Suggestions

1. Get into a pattern. We all love our catnaps every now and then but you should be careful with your internal clock. It's best to keep our brains and bodies on a schedule. Still, if you can't quit your naps (like me) try to have them around the same time of the day and for the same amount of time. Go for a refreshing 20 minute power nap instead of a lethargic two hours where you wake up more tired than you were before.

2. Power off. It can be quite jarring to go from being constantly accessible by cell phone, Facebook, and Skype to powering down everything— including our minds. Therefore, try to avoid Facebook stalking your ex-boyfriend or your frenemy right before bed (you don't want to have nightmares about either of those people, do you?) and give yourself at least a half hour before bed to just unwind and be with the people who are actually in your presence.

3. Be patient with yourself. Not everyone can be lucky when it comes to hitting the hay. Some people find the needle in the haystack more easily than others and needless to say, it can be a very frustrating process. Try to relax and be patient with yourself. It is what it is. Chances are, it's just one night and if it's an ongoing problem, seek advice from your doctor or try some natural remedies. Something as simple as sleeping shouldn't have the right to steal your happiness.

Healing Leads to Happiness

Just like any other age group, young adults face illness, disease, and accidents that can greatly take a jab at our happiness. We still hear the words, "you have cancer," "you will never walk again," or "you need surgery." It takes a lot of courage to not only hear these words when they're directed at you, but to then know how to respond with courage and resilience at such a young age. But as humans, we are blessed with a gift. Like Flubber, we do our best to bounce back no matter what we've been through. We may be molded temporarily, and it may become a part of us, but it never defines us indefinitely. We ultimately shape ourselves and decide who and how we want to be. Here's how some of you reacted when hard times hit.

Sunny Samples

1. Carmen: "I was in a terrible car accident. A few friends and I were driving to a party when a drunk driver hit us. I suffered from fractured

59

hips, a broken pelvis and ribs along with a sprained ankle. I feel so many different ways about what happened to me but most importantly, I am grateful to be alive and that my friends were safe. I still struggle with my happiness because I was used to looking a certain way and I didn't look the same after the accident. I gained some weight and was unable to work out as I once did. But things are getting better and I'm more and more happy every day."

2. George: "When I was two, I was diagnosed with non-Hodgkin's lymphoma. It came back when I was 14. I don't remember the treatments when I was two but I still vividly remember the treatments when I was 14. I also remember that I thought I was going to die. I have now been in remission for over 10 years. Cancer was a blessing and a curse but it shaped me into who I am today. It made me a very strong and grateful person. I learned that it is important to trust in your family and God and to know that they are looking out for you."

3. Kendall: "I sprained my back and had a herniated disc in the lower lumbar section of my spine. It hurt to walk, sit, and even lay down. I was miserable and in a lot of pain. I could not work, it was difficult to even go through school and I had to leave the sorority I was involved in because I had too many doctor's appointments to even have time to be in a club. I did not want to do anything or see anyone. I had to wear a brace for four months, get a shot in my spine, and take different medications. I also went through six weeks of physical therapy, 12 weeks of exercise physiology, and 12 weeks of pelvic floor physical therapy. Life was lonely and miserable."

Sunny Suggestion

I know how challenging it can be to feel happy when you're dealing with health issues. Just getting through the day is a goal in itself. But even when you're sick in bed or you're stuck in the hospital, the good news is that like our Flubber metaphor, humans have a natural tendency to adapt and revert to their baseline level of happiness. So if you consider yourself to be a naturally happy person, even the most challenging of experiences won't hold you down forever. If you're willing to perceive your setbacks as blessings in disguise, rather than something that will ruin your life forever, then happiness won't be far away.

Your Sunny Side: Have you ever been through a health hardship? How did it affect your happiness?

_____

_____

_____

How can you improve your mindset the next time you not feeling well?

_____

_____

Because there's only one incredible you, that means that you have only one body. You have to take care of it if you want to feel happy. Aeschylus, the Ancient Greek dramatist and playwright, was quoted as saying:

"Happiness is a choice that requires effort at times."

No one said it would be easy to pick the salad over the Slurpee, and no one denies that lying on the couch watching TV could be more relaxing than picking ourselves up and going to the gym. But these choices we make on a daily basis are decisions that later will ultimately lead to our level of happiness. It takes great dedication to choose a happiness that we will find in the future rather than a momentary second of pleasure. But if you are willing to love yourself enough to invest in a healthy diet, an exercise routine, and a good sleeping pattern, you will develop a healthy self-image that you can be proud of.

This can be a challenging chapter because our health is always on a continuum. We may be in great shape or maybe we need to lose some pounds. The problem comes when we base our self-worth on our reflection rather than our character. I hope that you can find a happiness that comes not from a number on a scale or a dress size. Instead, I hope you can find happiness from knowing that you are doing your best, despite what you weigh. We can't control everything in our life, but we can choose how we take care of ourselves. Love yourself in a way that makes you proud, regardless of the pounds. I know that no matter where you are in your life, whether you've just gone through a knee surgery or you've just splurged on an In n' Out burger, you can always bounce back and you can always bring happiness into your life. It's about loving who you are and living confidently in the body you have. I think you can do that. No wait. I know you can do that.

Get Your Goals
in High Gear

G raduate from college. Establish a career. Get married. Have kids. Sounds typical right? Well how about getting your Ph.D. in neuroscience, being the first female CEO of Disney, or writing your own New York Times bestselling book? Now that's more like it! Our generation is constantly setting goals for ourselves whether or not we verbalize it or write it down. We have learned to be dreamers; and if we put our mind to it, then nothing is impossible.

Yes, there may be limitations in time, money, and resources, but this shouldn't hinder us from striving for our full potential. These setbacks are nothing new. Take Dolly Parton; she's had 25 songs go to Number #1 on the billboard country charts, she manages Dolly Parton Enterprises (worth over $100 million), and she was even ranked #4 in CMT's "20 Sexiest Women in Country Music." (I'm sure those rhinestone dresses helped her out with that one…along with another asset). But did you know that Dolly was raised in a one-room cabin in Tennessee amongst 12 siblings? Her family had nothing but each other and Dolly had nothing but talent and faith. Yet even with a lack of the bacon, Dolly had the backbone to achieve her dreams because she didn't settle for anything less than success. She proved that there really is something to be said for working "9 to 5."

Just as Dolly didn't make excuses for the limitations she had in life, neither should we. Yet, many of us don't even know where to begin when asking ourselves that age old question: "So what exactly do I want to do with my life?" *And you don't know the answer?* Heaven forbid! Well, if it's any assurance, you don't need to know the answer. Besides, anyone who thinks they know it all often finds their equation doesn't come out quite as they planned. So it's okay if you don't know what you want to do with your life—you have time. As long as you're headed down a path you're proud of and working hard along the way, your happiness will ensue.

The best place to start is to realize that your goals will be ever-changing. This is your time for self-discovery—so why not have fun while doing it? Hopefully you will have fun throughout your entire life, but this is your chance to have an unabashed, carefree good time. (Minding that you obey the law!) This is your time to explore your world. And by the way, don't think for a second that taking this time for yourself is selfish—in fact, it's preemptively selfless because when you're doing what you love to do, the people around you will love being with you. Be so happy that you make others happy when they're with you.

What begins as fun for you will naturally lead to your life goals. I think Mary Poppins says it best: "In every job that must be done, there is an element of fun. And snap, the job's a game." Once you start incorporating the "fun factor" into your life, you'll see that you're working toward your goals instead of obligations—and you'll be so much happier along the way. If you start out with what makes you naturally happy, you will be all the more naturally inclined to set academic, career, and personal goals that are suited to your personal happiness and success.

But maybe you don't know where to begin. Or perhaps you feel overwhelmed by many dreams that seem impossible to actualize. There may be a surplus of setbacks when it comes to not only setting goals, but also to attaining them. Here is a list of some "clouds" that may be fogging up windows, along with some "defrosters" that will help you envision your goals and get them in high gear. Do you identify with any of these? Put a check by the ones that you can relate to.

Sunny Suggestions

_____ **Cloud #1**: My future looks like a Picasso painting. I'm so indecisive that I can't tell you whether I want to be an astronaut or an actress. I have no idea what I want to do with my life.

Defroster: Instead of feeling overwhelmed, try to feel grateful for your many interests. You are certainly not one to be pigeonholed. This is your time to try anything and everything that interests you; take classes that spark your curiosity, read books that detail someone's life you admire, and contact people who currently do what you want to do. You might be surprised by how welcoming people are when they hear that you want to learn from them. Most adults want to help you succeed.

Your Sunny Side: What can you do to start honing in on your interests?

_____

_____

_____ **Cloud #2**: I'd rather play SIMS all day and eat Ben and Jerry's round the clock. I don't feel motivated to take action unless that includes putting another 1,000 calories into my mouth.

Defroster: First, take a deep breath. We all have days like this when we just need to relax. But there's a limit. You can only pull the Scarlet O'Hara line: "I'll think about it tomorrow," for so long. If you don't start setting goals for yourself today, and continue to live a sedentary life, tomorrow will quickly turn you into the likes of a 40 year old with a potbelly and low self-esteem. So, to get yourself started, put down the stale popcorn and pick up some hobbies. Heck, when you're really ready write down some of your goals. Just acknowledging your dreams is a great start and you'll notice how happy you feel when you start making productivity a priority.

Eventually these small tasks will turn into bigger triumphs as you watch yourself succeed. You'll quickly learn that it feels much better to be successful than sedentary. Be patient with yourself though. It's okay to take gradual steps; even Neil Armstrong had to take one small step first when he landed on the moon. Eventually those small steps will turn into giant leaps and you'll feel so much more happy and satisfied with your life.

Your Sunny Side: What small steps can you take to get yourself motivated?

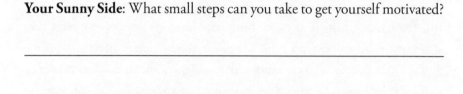

_____ **Cloud #3**: School, sports, friends, and family, and oh yeah, Facebook. There's no more time left in my day to fit something in like a far-fetched goal.

Defroster: Achieving goals certainly takes time. There will always be something that comes up. We are all so busy, but we still need to take the time to evaluate our priorities. You have to get real with yourself: Am I studying to become a lawyer or am I studying the subtle indentations on some cute boy's abs in their profile pic online? (Or if you're like me, looking up every recipe under the sun on Pinterest). Sometimes it's hard to admit, but maybe we need to focus on our self-improvement rather than analyzing how everyone else is doing. Pay attention to where you're actually putting your time.

Here's a good place to start: begin each week by focusing on one particular goal. Maybe you won't come close to finishing the task, but take time every day to do at least one thing that will get you one step closer. Let's say you want to get your SCUBA certification. Obviously you can't just jump in the ocean and start diving with the stingrays; but you can begin by researching where lessons are being taught and where some of the best places to dive would be. Remember that the turtle made it to the finish line before the hare. If you put in the dedication and the time, and most importantly if you have the will to do something, it can be done. Our greatest obstacles are often ourselves.

Your Sunny Side: What are three goals can you focus on?

1. _____

2. _____

3. _____

What are three time distracters that you struggle with?

1. _____

2. _____

3. _____

How can you prevent getting distracted by time wasters?

_____

_____

_____ **Cloud #4**: My dad's a math professor at Yale and my mom is a neurosurgeon from Harvard. I want to be a painter but if I don't set goals that are in alignment with my parents' wishes, then I'll be branded as the family failure.

Defroster: Many of us feel an immense amount of pressure from our parents. But this is not necessarily a bad thing; it just means that your parents are deeply invested in your future and they want you to do well. I think most parents want their children to be happy; sometimes they just don't realize that your dreams may be different than their dreams *for you*. But you have to remember (and they can be kindly reminded) that you are becoming an adult. This means you have a personal responsibility to yourself to see to it that you are happy.

If your parents won't budge on the dreams they have for you versus the dreams you have for yourself, try to explain how much their support means towards fulfilling your goals. More than anything, you have to advocate for your happiness. If there's no possible compromise, try to make an effort to see the benefits of what they want you to study, learn, or try; there is always something to appreciate. And if you're absolutely miserable trying out their plan for your life, then remember, that their roof doesn't have to stay over your head forever.

Quite often, parents just have a practical mindset. They want their children to live comfortably and they think that this may come only with safe, sure-bet careers. But maybe you don't like to play it safe. I'm a token example; you can imagine how thrilled my dad was when he heard I wanted to be a motivational speaker and author. "That's great Lauren, but what about making money?" Oh yeah, about that. It all depends on what you want for your life, but for me, I discovered that if I'm happy with what I'm doing, I know that I have a much better shot at success than living a miserable life in a cubicle only to fulfill my dad's plan. If there's anything I've learned, it's that if you don't love what you do, it's much harder to love your life. Of course we all have to make sacrifices and life throws its fair share of curveballs, but if you can follow you dream, dare to be brave enough to go for it—don't let anyone hold you back.

Your Sunny Side: What can you do to negotiate with your parents so that they can see how important your dreams are to you?

_____

_____

_____ **Cloud #5:** I know that I want to help save the pandas in China. I feel extremely passionate about this cause but I don't know how I can financially support such an endeavor. Is the money supposed to grow off the bamboo? Because it's definitely not coming out of my bank account any time soon.

Defroster: Money is a huge hardship for young adults. You are either strapped to your parent's wallets like a kid on one of those ridiculous monkey leashes or you are probably shelling out your paychecks either on some elaborate dinner to impress your date or gosh nabbit, to pay for that parking ticket you got last month (trust me, those things aren't cheap). Saving can seem like the last thing on your mind when you are just struggling to pay for the day-to-day necessities.

So if you do earn an income, be sure to have a bank account where you can strive to save at least 10% every month (but the more, the better!) And if you're still stuck in your mama kangaroo's money pouch, then be respectful of how you spend your parents' money and be mindful of your parents' hard work. No matter what your financial situation, it's best to think twice before you make a purchase. Always ask yourself: "Will this make me happy today?" More importantly, "Will this make me happy a month from now, a year from now?" So the next time you want to buy another café latte or get a pedicure, remember the goals you've set and ask yourself whether you'd rather have the money go towards a momentary splurge or a lifelong memory or experience. Your choice.

Your Sunny Side: How can you be smarter about your spending so that you can reach goals that mean something to you?

_____ **Cloud #6**: My best friend just learned how to speak Italian in Florence and my boyfriend just got in to an Ivy League law school. How I am supposed to live up to that? I feel like I'll never be able to make my mark.

Defroster: It can be easy to feel like you don't measure up, but instead of feeling jealous, let someone else's experiences motivate you that much more. I know it can feel like the competition is just too much to live up to, but know this: you have your own unique talents and skills that make you shine. Focus on what makes you great rather than what makes others good. And don't be too afraid or too proud to ask for help from the people around you who are succeeding. You can gain so much free wisdom by letting others teach you what they already know. Let's start seeing the competition as camaraderie.

Your Sunny Side: How can you start seeing others success as an opportunity to motivate rather than devalue yourself?

_____

_____

_____ **Cloud #7**: I'm ready to turn my "Teenage Dream" into a reality—I want to be a professional singer. Watch out Katy Perry! Now how do I get someone to actually listen and give me a chance?

Defroster: It may be daunting to know where to begin with a tremendous goal, especially if your goal depends on whom you know, where you are, and if you have luck on your side. So take fate into your own hands. Be proactive and search for every possible opportunity; don't wait for the right people or the right connections to come your way—I hate to tell you, but chances are they won't.

Find success by making yourself a success. Invest in yourself. Most importantly, as a young adult, don't be daunted by your age or by your lack of experience. If anything, use these things to your advantage. The younger you are, the more impressive you will be if you can pull it off. My acting teacher, Leonora Gershman-Pitts, told me that if you can't find work, then create work for yourself. While I'm no longer a starry-eyed actor, I've now applied this principle to writing this book. Through this process I have learned that you, and you alone, can create your own success. Of course, it takes others to continue your success but the foundation is built with your hands.

Your Sunny Side: What steps can YOU take to make your dreams come true?

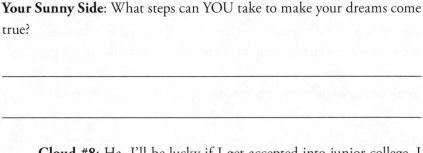

_____ **Cloud #8**: Ha, I'll be lucky if I get accepted into junior college. I think I'll have to forge my admissions acceptance letter just so my parents will stop asking about it.

Defroster: So maybe you don't have the best academic track record. Or maybe you didn't make the soccer team. But it is never too late to turn your life around. I know how college admissions can be disheartening; your application is thrown left or right depending on a series of letters and numbers that are supposed to define you. I know it's not always fair. You can't control everything but start out with what you *can* control. This doesn't apply to just college admissions, but to any try-out in life; whether it's an audition, a job interview, or a first date. It has been said that you have a good two seconds to make a first impression, so make those seconds count. Prove to people that you are worth their time by expressing confidence, but not cockiness. But before you can do this, you need to prove to *yourself* that you are entirely worth *your* time.

Until you can love yourself for who you are, you'll be hard pressed to be happy. And until you give that love to yourself, that you so rightly deserve, no college acceptance letter can give you the true happiness that you desire. The ink will fade on the paper and so will your happiness unless you realize that your life is more than a bunch of "yeses" and "no's." True happiness can only start with self-acceptance.

Furthermore, remember that people can only judge you as much as you let them. Try not to take peoples' decisions personally and remember that everything happens for a reason. Instead of asking, "Why did this happen to me?" ask, "What am I supposed to learn from this?" Maybe you needed a wake-up call. Maybe you needed to take a leap of faith. Maybe you needed to be guided in a new direction. Whatever it is that you need, take your circumstances and the feedback from others and use it as fuel for a better future. Even the broken road can be blessed. Thank you Rascal Flatts.

Your Sunny Side: What can you do to improve your self-worth?

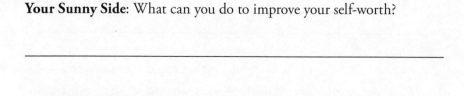

_____ **Cloud #9**: I just got my degree in chemical engineering but I think I want to get into real estate (sound similar to the late Lakers owner, Jerry Buss?). If you're thinking about a major life change and wondering, did I just waste four years and $100,000 of my life? No, you didn't! Read further.

Defroster: I wouldn't be a member of this generation if I didn't like *Twilight* at least a little. More than Jacob's tanned, carved-out contour of a body or Edward's whipped cream, wonder-boy hair, I remember Jessica's graduation speech in *Eclipse*. Okay, I lied, I remember the body and the hair more but still, her words struck a chord with me.

She said, "This isn't the time to make hard and fast decisions, it's time to make mistakes. Major in philosophy 'cause there's no way to make a career out of that. Change your mind. Then change it again, because nothing is permanent."

Now of course, most of our parents don't have the piggy banks to send us through college twice (many don't have the funds to send us once). Besides, I'm not really sure you want to go through the whole process again as a 25 year old surrounded by fresh-faced nineteen year olds. But, just as Jessica said, you can change your mind. Over 60% of college students switch their major at least once and often three or four times. I had one of my stints as a business economics major; boy was that short-lived. There's no need to feel trapped by the initial decisions you make or goals you set. Life changes and you won't be happy until you can learn to accept it.

Instead of punishing yourself, take pride in the decisions you make. It can be easy to self-deprecate and hate yourself for what you think may have been a wrong turn in your life. It wasn't. Those classes, that ex-boyfriend, or that road trip you got lost on only made you a stronger, smarter person with more life experiences to learn from. Take that knowledge and move on with your life to bigger and better things. Goals aren't set in stone, they're meant to help you set up a happy life.

Your Sunny Side: How can you come to appreciate and learn from some of the decisions in your life that you have previously seen as regrets or mistakes?

_____

_____

_____ **Cloud #10**: So I want to swim with sharks but I'm scared to death that wow, my leg might actually get bitten off. How can I set goals and still be safe at the end of the day?

Defroster: Whether it is a physical fear, or a fear like "stage fright," fear can be one of the most debilitating handicaps when it comes to accomplishing our goals—especially the ones that challenge us emotionally, physically, and/or mentally. But you set these goals for a reason. It is because you know that they will make you better, stronger, and ultimately, a happier person.

I love Des Brown's quote: "Too many of us are not living our dreams because we are living our fears." But don't you want to live your dreams instead? So see what's waiting for you in the world...from a shark tank, an engine-sputtering safari cruiser, or an open-door airplane. Or maybe your adventurous side awaits you from your college dorm that is 2,000 miles from home, your new apartment in Tokyo, or your meditation ashram in India. Live outside of your comfort zone. It's not so much where you are or what you're doing...it's a way of living.

Your Sunny Side: What are three fears you have that are preventing you from your goals?

_____

_____

What can you do to start overcoming these fears?

_____

_____

Make a Game Plan if You Plan to Win

So why am I such a big advocate of goal setting, and as a consequence, organization? Because it not only makes us happy when we are ready for life, it makes so many other people happy too. If you want to see your goals become a reality, you've got to use your organizational skills to plan accordingly. When we are punctual and prepared, we are helping others and ourselves in the process. Even if we take just a few extra minutes to write down our goals and obligations, everyone can benefit. Think about the times when you didn't plan ahead or you simply forgot. Remember the look of disappointment on your friend's face when you forgot her birthday or the fine you had to pay when you didn't show up to your meeting? When we don't pay attention to our plans, no matter how big or small, we not only let ourselves down, we unintentionally let so many others down in the process.

Many young adults are already setting goals and writing them down on a daily basis. It's part of their daily routine because they realize how much natural happiness it brings to their life.

Sunny Samples

1. Gabby: "I set small goals every day. Among other things, I run a little longer than the day before, write another page for my essay, and do something nice for my mom. I feel good about myself when I make the people around me happy."

2. Julianne: "I have always set goals for myself. Quite honestly, my motivation comes from seeing the people in their 30's who have no idea what they want to do with their lives—the people who have no job or education. That would be my worst nightmare."

3. Megan: "I try to make the goals that I set pretty high. I believe that it is important to work for what you want. I do not let myself take the easy path in life. It may be a struggle, but when you fail, it only makes you come back stronger the next time you try!"

So now that the fog has lifted and you've seen the light, you may be wondering where that light is headed. Perhaps you have a vision of your goals, but they are not clearly defined or organized. So I'd like to emphasize some of the greatest tips that I have learned through personal experience, research, and collaboration.

Sunny Suggestions

1. **Write a to-do list on most days**. Whether you prefer to write your list when you wake up or the evening before when you go to bed, make note of the things you need to accomplish in the day ahead. If you're like me, you can write down the most minute tasks, but on the whole you should make note of two things: goals that *need* to get done and responsibilities that should *ideally* get done. No matter how detailed or brief, making your list on a regular basis teaches you how to prioritize your time and plan ahead.

And don't be down on yourself if you don't get everything done. In fact, if I accomplish 50% of my goals for the day, then that's a day well spent. That being said, keep your goals within reason. For example, don't say that you will run 15 miles when you're barely able to run for 15 minutes. Be gentle with yourself otherwise you'll set yourself up for failure.

Here is an example of one of my daily to-do lists to get you going on your own list:

1. _____ Make a list (just kidding!)
2. _____ Respond to emails; get inbox down to 75 emails.
3. _____ Clean room and house. Iron dad's shirts and do laundry.
4. _____ Write blog post and 5 Daily Gratitudes.
5. _____ Edit book for an hour.
6. _____ Go to psychology meeting at 4:00 pm.
7. _____ Attend life science lecture at 12:15 pm.
8. _____ Buy present for Kelly's birthday.
9. _____ Go bowling with friends at 9:00 pm.
10. ____ Fill out paperwork for internship.

You'll also notice that my list is not necessarily in order of time or priority. I even jot down things that I know will get completed regardless of whether I write them down or not (like attending my lecture and meeting). Regardless of different events being mandatory or not, I find that a checklist holds you more accountable. With this increased accountability you'll soon see that you accomplish much more in your day and you'll be more motivated when you know exactly what you need to complete for the day. And once you *do* finish what you've set out to do, you can't help but be happy with yourself for following through.

However you decide to make your list, be sure to carry this list with you throughout the day; it can be easy to forget about some of the smaller "to do's" when you're out and about. I usually write my list on a little notepad so that I can conveniently carry it around in my bag and glance at it periodically. This is a great way to free you from all the mental clutter holding you back from the task at hand. Putting it on paper puts away your unnecessary stress and instead puts your happiness at the forefront.

You'll notice I suggest writing a list on "most days." Sometimes, you need a day off to clear your mental bank. So cash out and have a day for yourself. Checklists are great when you're on a "worker-bee" mode but sometimes you need a "queen-bee" mode. Give yourself that freedom and enjoy the honey you earned from your hard work.

Your Sunny Side: What are some of your daily goals that you can start writing down?

_____

_____

2.   **Get a calendar and have fun with it.** Like animals? Like picturesque settings? If you like *something*, then believe me, there is a calendar for it. Pick one that you'll enjoy looking at and put it in a place where you'll see it on a daily basis. A calendar is essential because it is so visual—you just can't miss it, especially if you love the picture on it. I personally love kittens and seeing those squinty, soft faces every morning always makes me wake up with a smile.

Also, it can give you a spatial context of time that a planner or a blackberry can fumble for. You can clearly see when that deadline is coming up and you undoubtedly know when your Aunt Mae's birthday will be—it's all there. You can plan accordingly because you know what's coming in the days, weeks, and months ahead. You'll see that your baseline happiness will surprisingly increase when you start prepping for your days ahead. When you plan your life to the best of your ability, you can plan on a life of happiness because you're prepared for it.

3.   **Keep a planner or use technology to organize your schedule.** Most people don't carry their calendars in their purses. Sometimes there are important dates or notices that come up and you need to write them down immediately. Use a planner or your cell phone to make note of these time worthy tidbits so that you won't be caught off guard later. Cell phones can be especially handy tools because you can program them to send reminders as often as you need them.

The Sunny Set

I've suggested keeping a list of goals, a "to-do" list, a planner, and a calendar. What do all of these things have in common? You write everything down! This applies to **The Sunny Set** as well. What is a Sunny Set? It's similar to a "Bucket List," but with a little different perspective. Rather than a list of things to do before you die, it's a list of goals to accomplish while you're living. Once we have defined our goals, we can begin working toward them on an ongoing, daily basis. This list will grow, change, and develop throughout the years. As you grow, so will your goals.

Your goals should challenge, inspire, and motivate you to live your life to the fullest on a daily basis. Whether you have a list or not, I'm guessing you have at least a rough idea of what you'd like to achieve in your life. So if you only have a few ideas or you've made a list of hundreds of goals, now is the perfect time to create your Sunny Set and get started!

There are so many benefits to putting your Sunny Set in print. You'll see an added element of happiness in your life once you know both the significant and simple things you'd like to achieve. Writing them down is the first step toward accomplishing your goal because it's an act of commitment. The next step is sharing your list with the people you love. You're admitting to yourself and to others that you have dreams that are valid. You are acknowledging that you have potential and that you believe in yourself. Putting faith in yourself like this is an immediate way to increase your self-esteem and your inner sense of joy. You'll start feeling more excited to live your life.

No goal is too small and no goal is too big. I have listed my personal Sunny Set in the appendix so you can get a little inspiration when making your own list. I recommend writing your initial list during one sitting when you're feeling especially creative and then keeping it in a special place where you can refer to it frequently. I wrote mine in a journal and I add to it often. I keep it by my bedside and now it's online for the whole world to see so that it's a constant reminder for me. If you want to not only set goals, but also to succeed at them, you'll need to have your Sunny Set in clear sight. Type your list. Make a poster. Decorate it. However if you would like to be reminded of your goals, make sure you're seeing your Sunny Set on a daily basis.

I know it may be daunting to share your personal dreams with other people, but take pride in your Sunny Set. It shows that you have passion, motivation, and optimism. You might be surprised by how supportive your family and friends are; in fact, you'll probably inspire them to create a Sunny Set of their own. The more you share your goals, the more ideas you'll come up with and the best part is, you'll often find a friend who wants to achieve many of the same goals as you. After all, who wants to ride donkeys in the Grand Canyon by themselves or go skydiving solo?

You may think that a Sunny Set is selfish. Setting goals for YOU and all the dedicated time it takes to achieve them may seem like a self absorbed notion. It is actually selfless if it's done right. While it is an investment in yourself, the happiness you derive from achieving your goals will transform others as well. When you're happy, you're offering a tremendous gift to the people around you because chances are, you'll help them experience their own happiness as well. Happiness is rarely lonely; it's too contagious to not reach out to other people. You'll find that going for your goals is about one of the fastest ways to spread the happiness bug. Here are some Sunny Samples to remind you of how great it feels to get your goals done.

Sunny Samples

1. Taylor: "I ran cross country in middle school and high school. I remember my very first cross-country race in my new high school in Lakeland, Michigan. I was the only freshman girl that came from White Lake middle school to run Lakeland cross country. All the other girls came from the rival middle school, Oak Valley. Despite an entire summer of running with these 'rival' girls, we still had yet to strike up a friendship. The big race day came and I was running along with three other freshman girls from the rival Oak Valley. The gun was shot and before I knew it I was in third place. The race ended and as I ran into the cross-country chute I couldn't see anything, my legs were wobbly, and I couldn't breathe...this is normal after running a great race. I found out that I had been my team's third finisher and first place freshman! I ran Varsity my first race and beat my rival teammates! I felt on top of the world. To receive recognition from my coach and the other girls was the best feeling. Even better was that I made Varsity and ran a great race as a freshman, accomplishing a goal I thought would be nearly impossible."

2.   Jamie: "Until you experience it, achieving a goal is one of those feelings that you can never understand. Once you feel it, you think to yourself, 'Oh, so that's why people work so hard toward their goals!' It truly is a different type of happiness. Doing good deeds for others brings happiness to yourself but when it's your hard work for your personal goals, that also brings a special happiness. It means that you don't have to depend on others to make you happy...you did it yourself."

3.   Amy: "Going to Africa has been on my list of things to do since I started learning about Africa during my sophomore year of high school. After having all of my African Studies courses under my belt now (as a junior in college), it was really exciting to actually experience and witness concepts that I've learned. The trip was also such a landmark for my future goals because I always have said that I want to join Doctors Without Borders; but how could I know I wanted to be a travelling doctor without previously having traveled out of the United States? Now, I know without a doubt that I'm more than capable of the career I've dreamed about. Don't ever be scared to go for an adventure just because others don't understand your goals or you feel overwhelmed by misleading fears. Do what you believe in and you will not be let down. Be open and adventurous. Let yourself be inspired and be inspiring to others."

Sunny Suggestions

1.   **Get ready to write!** To write your Sunny Set, find a journal or a notebook; you can even type it on your laptop. Just make sure it's somewhere visible and easily accessible. And then, just write. No need to censor yourself. If you want to meet the President, then go for it! No dream

is too big, too risky, or too bold. Now obviously I'm not encouraging you to write down anything illegal, indecent, or harmful to others; come up with a list that you think will add to your happiness in life. It might help to break your list into various components. Here are a few ideas to get you started:

Travel:
1. Eat gelato in Italy.
2. Kiss a dolphin in Hawaii.
3. Hold a koala in Australia.

Fitness:
1. Run the Disneyland half-marathon.
2. Be able to bench press 100 pounds.
3. Climb Mount Whitney.

Academic:
1. Get into a great university. Keep a few specific ones in mind.
2. Graduate with honors and a 3.8 GPA.
3. Major in physiological science.

Your Sunny Side: To get you started, what are 10 goals you would like to achieve in your lifetime?

1. _____

2. _____

3. _____

4. _____

5. _____

6. _____

7. _____

8. _____

9. _____

10. _____

2. Personalize it. When you look at my Sunny Set, you'll notice that I comment on each goal that I have achieved or attempted. Be sure to do this for yourself. It emphasizes the experience and you'll learn how you can improve in the future if you weren't successful at a particular goal the first time. It's also nice to leave a little memory for yourself by writing a specific detail about the experience. It's an added benefit if you want to keep a little memento from each goal you achieve.

3. Focus on one goal a week. Your brain will shut down if you try to juggle snorkeling in the Cayman Islands, working for Vogue, and graduating from Harvard all in one week. Instead, focus on a specific goal that you can take tiny bites out of. Think of it like a box of chocolates; you'd feel sick if you ate the whole box at once but it's a special treat when you have just one piece a day. The same applies to goals. Only bite off as much as you can chew.

Your Sunny Side: What are three goals that you specifically want to start working on?

1. _____

2. _____

3. _____

4. Put your goals everywhere. What's the picture on your desktop? What are the posters on your wall? Don't let yourself forget about your goals—make them readily visible. You can even make a "Dream Board." Go through all of your favorite magazines and paste pictures of your dream home, your dream car, your dream job, etc. Watch your dreams become a reality. Pinterest—an amazing website if you haven't seen it yet—is another great way to make your goals visual.

Your Sunny Side: How can you make your goals more visible?

_____

_____

5. Encourage yourself. Talk nicely to yourself. When you send yourself an email, tell yourself that you're doing a great job. Post sticky notes that have inspiring phrases on them. Keep cards that have kind words written on them and go through them from time to time. These little pieces of positive encouragement will keep you going when you're feeling discouraged. Many of the best goals require bravery in the midst of setbacks.

Your Sunny Side: What can you do to give yourself some positive praise?

_____

_____

Starting Back Up Even When You Strike Out

Remember that not every goal you attempt will be a homerun. Take hatching my chicken eggs as an example. I tried to no avail to see those little eggs hatch; I bought the incubator, had the eggs shipped, and I nurtured those eggs with diligence on a daily basis for over three weeks. But they still didn't hatch. A year later, I repeated this process with the same results. Even so, it doesn't mean I won't keep trying. I'm intent on someday seeing my little chicks hatch!

And while some dreams can be dreamt again and again, and tried again and again, some are once in a lifetime chances that you can't get back. But just because you don't necessarily "win," "finish," or "succeed," doesn't mean that you failed. If you tried and gave it your best effort, then it is a job well done, even if you didn't get the medal, plaque, or end result you wanted. Here's what you told me about your accomplishments that didn't actualize.

Sunny Samples

1. Justin: "There were times in high school that I didn't make a play or I got a bad grade. It made me feel like I totally missed what I had set out to accomplish. For a little while I would pout about it, but then I would remember that everything happens for a reason and I would just have to work harder next time."

2. Tia: "Even though I have unwavering amounts of determination and strength, it would be crazy to believe that I will accomplish every goal I set. Nearly all my life I have had a goal to get a puppy. All I ever wanted for every birthday, Christmas, or special occasion, was a dog of my own. My parents never let me get one and as I got older and started working and driving, I realized that all I had to do was go to the shelter and pick up one. (I'm sure my parents would be angry with me but I doubt that they would make me return a homeless dog.) I came to this realization about the same time I realized that I really do not have time to take care of another being. I travel on my own annually about twice a year and I am crazy busy going to school, work, and everything else. It would be irresponsible for me to try to take care of a dog while being so busy. So my goal, my dream, my wish of getting a puppy won't be accomplished for a good couple of years. I guess I haven't failed but I haven't accomplished my goal either. But I'm not giving up!"

3. Natalia: "I have goals that were not met. It makes me sad but I will always try to get as close to my goal as I possibly can. Failure is not an option for me. When I do succeed in fulfilling my aspirations it makes me so happy. Because happiness is such an important part of my life I will always keep trying."

My Sunny Side

I remember I wanted to speak at my high school graduation and even though I prepared thoroughly and auditioned, I was not selected. And I'm ok with that. Sure it was disappointing but I just moved on to the next goal. The fact is, I did everything possible on my end to accomplish that goal, and then I let fate decide. If I know in my heart that I've done my best, then I can be assured that it simply wasn't meant to be. Rather than fester in frustration, I prefer to learn from the experience and then move on to the next goal. There are bigger fish to fry and more happiness to be had.

I know it can be easier said than done. Many young adults told me they feel "ashamed" and "hurt" and that their self esteem really takes a hit when they have been unsuccessful at a goal. That's completely understandable; any form of rejection can be taken personally if we let it. But we need to remember that we are part of a bigger picture where sometimes we need to be leaders, and sometimes we need to be followers. Sometimes we need to excel, and sometimes we need to struggle. Take Albert Einstein's words, "Anyone who has never made a mistake has never tried anything new."

So even though there may be a risk of non-achievement, take the chance to try something new. Even if it scares the living daylights out of you and even if, at first, it might make you feel alone. I love how Tessa put it, "I haven't failed. I think that many goals just take time to accomplish. Even if you think you have failed maybe you just need to approach your goal differently or at a different time."

Sunny Suggestion

Find out what you're afraid of and then face it. So much of the time we are deathly afraid of being told, "NO." But depending on your *perspective*, even a "NO" equates to a "YES" in other ways. As they say, when one door closes, another opens (or many!) As my mentor Lisa Bloom says, "If you never ask, the answer will *always* be no." So you have to ask, you have to try, and you have to take chances. While you may be temporarily unhappy if someone does tell you "no," you're going to be ten times more unhappy if you never ask in the first place. Don't let yourself hold you back.

Your Sunny Side: What are three fears in your life that are holding you back?

1. _____

2. _____

3. _____

How can you combat these fears?

_____

_____

Take a Chance on Me

The greatest goals often take the greatest risks. The greatest (and wisest) risks lead to the greatest rewards. I don't think we're taking enough beneficial risks and that's part of the reason we're not as happy as we would like to be. Before I continue, let me clarify what "risk" means in this context. Here are some examples of what I'm talking about: taking challenging courses for the sake of learning even though you could get a lower grade, venturing to a foreign country even if you're worried you'll be homesick, or trying a new food even though you're nervous you won't like the taste. I'm not referring to the risks people take with experimental drug use, unsafe sexual encounters, or anything of that nature. I am the Sunny Girl after all! I would never advocate those kinds of risk because they rarely, if ever, add to your happiness. We keep it clean here.

So many of us choose comfort over risk because we have a wrong connotation of the word. When many of us think of the "risk," we think of impending failure, doom, and inescapable fear. But taking a risk doesn't necessarily have to be frightening, it can be exciting. A risk can represent an opportunity for personal improvement, strength of character, and ultimate happiness. If we choose our risks wisely, so that they challenge us without defeating us, we can expect to live our lives in a new light. So here are a few risk takers who aren't afraid to live on the unpredictable side.

Sunny Samples

1.   Marianne: "I'm taking a risk by going to an out of state college, Texas. I don't know anyone who lives there and the culture is extremely different. But I'm happy to be taking a chance and it's exciting to move out and be on my own. I know I won't have anyone but myself to rely on and that's okay."

2.   Hailey: "The end of my long distance high school relationship was messy. It left me with many trust issues and a fear of committing to someone again. Luckily for me, the next man in my life was the best boyfriend a girl could ask for. The only problem was that it was another long distance relationship, and I mean *really* long distance. I live in California and he was going to school in New York and traveling to places like South Korea on a regular basis. I would only get to see him once every four months or so, and then only for a few weeks at a time. Despite all of this I took the risk and we ended up having a very happy relationship. Even though we are no longer together I owe a big part of the happy person I am today to that relationship."

3.   Jessie: "This past summer I studied abroad in Spain. I was nervous about embarking on this adventure with a group of students from across the United States, of which I only knew one person. I was nervous that I wouldn't make friends, that I wouldn't like my homestay family, that the language would be too difficult, and that I would be homesick. However, this trip proved to be one of the best experiences of my life. I learned to

live like a local, greatly improve my Spanish, and made memories to last a lifetime. I look back on the trip with a strong sense of happiness and satisfaction, and I am so glad I took the risk to go abroad."

Sunny Suggestion

Be bold and brave. Perhaps we hold back because every time we take a risk we are allowing ourselves to be vulnerable. We are opening ourselves for judgment. We could be wrong, we could be laughed at, or we could be shunned. But in actuality, this is rarely the case. The truth is, people will respect you so much more when they see you taking risks, even when you don't get the intended outcome you hoped for. Most people don't have the courage to pursue their dreams whole-heartedly. When people see that you aren't afraid to go after your goals, they may not only be surprised, but also impressed by your tenacity and your courage to succeed. Chances are, you'll inspire others to take their own healthy risks as well.

Your Sunny Side: What can you do to start taking more healthy risks that will increase your happiness?

_____

_____

Enjoy Your Ride

Here is my chosen quote for this chapter. Hopefully it will get you excited about getting started with your goals.

"Success is a journey, not a destination. The doing is often more important than the outcome." –Arthur Ashe.

This is why we must live for the minutes in our day that will eventually become the years of our lives. I know how easy it can be to complain or give up on a goal when it gets challenging. You might not be feeling so happy when you need to play the piano for an hour a day or do that twentieth pirouette that you still probably won't land just yet. But you have to keep trying and find the joy in your struggle. Be in the moment. Know that you have it within you. Your courage and your motivation to keep trying speaks volumes about your character. Because in the end, no matter how talented or intelligent you may be, dedication is ultimately the factor that will turn your goal into an achievement and your happiness into a reality.

Sunshine for the Soul

As I said in the introduction, true happiness isn't solely based on material possessions. It's much more than the Lamborghinis, the Louis Vuitton's, and having the house on the hill that many of us dream about. Instead, true happiness is about our relationships—one of the most important, being our relationship with ourselves. For some of us, that relationship extends to a Higher Power. I think our faith and spirituality are key components to our happiness and many of my fellow writers think so as well.

Before I continue, I want to be clear about how I am defining "spiritual." It may mean being in touch with God and your religion but it could also mean being in touch with your sense of self. The word carries a broad definition because our generation has a broad spectrum of beliefs, whether or not they are influenced by religion. Yet no matter what our individual beliefs are, spirituality has the potential to offer us a sense of peace that is untouchable, a contentment that is incomparable, and a whole new level of happiness. Our spirituality helps us survive through our most challenging experiences but it also helps us thrive in our happiest and most joyful times.

I hope you'll keep an open mind throughout this chapter. Be open to new faiths, new ideas, and even new possibilities within your own sense of spirituality. I believe in tolerance, but also in acceptance and understanding and I hope you will join me in this mindset. This book is meant to be shared by everyone, of all faiths, backgrounds, and walks of life—no matter what our individual spirituality is like, happiness is universal.

There was a resounding response from young adults who wanted to write about how their spirituality has affected their happiness. More than talking about boyfriends or puppies, this is what happiness means to them.

Sunny Samples

1. Jamie: "Knowing who I am, where I came from, and where I am going gives me a wonderful sense of security and purpose in life. Without this, life would not have the same meaning and it would be difficult living only for the moment and for temporary satisfaction. I believe that life is not only about finding happy moments, but working towards eternal joy. I think that if we learn to sacrifice and give of ourselves in this life, there will be great rewards in the life to come."

2. Drew: "I am an extremely spiritual person--I consider my relationship with God to be the most important thing in my life. This relationship and my spirituality are key players in my happiness. I have yet to find something that counters negativity in my life with the same force as taking a moment away from it all, and engaging in my spirituality--usually through a conversation with God. This relationship helps me enjoy and appreciate my happiness, and it gives me perspective to overcome times in my life that are less than happy."

3. Aubrey: "Being a spiritual person gives my life purpose. I believe that someone is watching over me, and actually cares about my feelings on a grander scale than the people in my life. I am able to feel content and happy with my life, even when it is less than ideal. I am able to relax and know that in the end, everything will come together for the good. That leaves me with a peace that many people do not understand. I would not be happy just living life for the sake of taking up space. Believing in God gives me a greater purpose, and a hope that allows me to be happy, even in the most trying times."

4.   Taylor: "Every day I try to become more and more spiritually minded. I try to read scriptures, write in my journal, and find my own Garden of Eden where I can seek peace in a quiet place all to myself. I constantly try to find the good in life, the good in people, and the good in myself, and I try to improve every hour of every day. I try to go to church on Sundays but more importantly, I try to implement the things I'm taught during the services throughout the week. I strive to lead by example by serving others. In doing so I serve myself a helping of happiness!"

5.   April: "I try to stay in constant communication with God. I have never regarded Him as some relentless, hostile being who wants me to beg for a scrap of His attention. I believe God wants to participate in our everyday lives, and I don't think He regards any problem as too insignificant. Even when I hear a siren on the street, I send up a prayer for whoever is lying in that ambulance. I set aside time to focus on Him, but I also try to make my life a constant prayer."

I am truly inspired by my peers' faith in a greater purpose beyond themselves. While our spiritual beliefs may bring happiness, it hopefully will bring something even more powerful: *joy.* Joy is the type of happiness that maintains an inner peace in spite of one's circumstances. Contrary to what some may think, joy and happiness don't necessarily need to be two separate ideas. Unfortunately, modern America has belittled happiness by identifying it as a somewhat frilly and frivolous notion of shallow bliss. In my opinion, happiness can be the equivalent of joy: a resounding, all-encompassing, ever-present, sense of well-being. Happiness doesn't have to be momentary if we are finding it in the right places—and when it comes from our spirituality, we are definitely headed in the right direction.

Here's **My Sunny Side**: I was the girl who grew up in the church. I sang in the choir and I was a regular attendee. But my spirituality may not have gotten packed up with the iPod and laptop when I moved away to college. I was happy in my day-to-day activities, but I didn't always make time for my relationship with God. I was happy enough, but I didn't have the resounding joy that I knew I could have. It made me think, is it easier to just be comfortably "happy" rather than deeply "joyful"? Sometimes I think the answer is "yes." It's more convenient, more practical. It can be easier and safer, but is it better?

No, it's not better—at least not in the long run. We need to take on the challenge of joy, not just the task of happiness because as much as I love the little birds that flit outside my window, there's something that stirs in my heart's window—my soul. It's easy to look at what's outside, but we need to start looking inside.

One of the greatest challenges I face, and many of you probably struggle with as well, is simply making time for your spirituality—it can be hard work. It's more challenging than glazing over Facebook for an hour or mindlessly texting ten people at once. But it's so incredibly worth it. When we are committed to being spiritually healthy, we can be spiritually happy. Don't you want a happiness that's untouchable? I do. And as much as I love making schedules and daily checklists, spirituality is not something to be penciled in, it is a practice to be inked into our way of life. Instead of adding it to our "to-do-list," we should have our spirituality so deeply ingrained in our identity that we take it with us wherever we go.

As a Christian, there are many different sermons I've heard and verses I've read but there is one idea that has stayed with me no matter how far I may stray. It's the thought that your relationship with God is like a seed; once it has been planted in you it never truly leaves you. Even though you may go through droughts or storms in your life, the seed stays in your soul. While my faith may falter or my courage collapse, I take comfort knowing that my relationship with God will always be in my life. Whether near or far, it never leaves me. I'm able to live a happier life knowing that God will always be within me.

Sunny Suggestions

1. Carve out time for your spirituality: If you're not already incorporating your spirituality in your life, start by carving out some time in your day to focus on your beliefs. It might seem unnatural at first, but you'll notice yourself feeling more content and at ease in your life when you have a strong sense of your spirituality.

Your Sunny Side: How can you make time to strengthen your spirituality?

_____

_____

2. Do your daily devotion. As much as I love Daily Devotionals, I'm recommending a daily devotion to your faith, however you see fit. No matter what you decide, it takes practice, discipline and diligence. For some studying their spirituality may come naturally, but we all need to dedicate time to go beyond the surface level of our lives and connect with our spirit. I know that I often get caught up in daily routine and trials but there are moments when I find myself needing to just pause. To be still. Happiness is a shallow pool if you don't go deeper into your spirituality.

Your Sunny Side: Do you think you're dedicating enough time for your spirituality? Why?

_____

_____

How can you make more time for your spirituality and what will you do during this time?

_____

_____

3. Connect beyond the small talk. One of the best things I did during my college career was to join a Bible study group. It was so refreshing to have conversations that didn't revolve around gossip, social gatherings, and complaining. Intellectual and spiritual conversations are the healthy foods our mind needs. No matter what your faith, having stimulating talks that challenge and strengthen your beliefs is so important. You form deeper conversations, evolve new ideas, and grow stronger in your values. I always felt rejuvenated after going to bible study and I think you too will feel renewed if you participate in more spiritual talks.

A Starved Spirituality?

I take comfort in the fact that I am not alone. Whether it is the people of this world or whatever is out there that is not of this world, we are surrounded by love if we choose to embrace it. Sometimes we deny ourselves this love; it can be out of guilt, out of shame, or out of rebellion. Some young adults may get the idea that they are unworthy when they're subjected to the stereotype that our generation can be rebellious, disrespectful or disconnected. But just because some of us may have a hair color that may be a primary color (aka red or blue) it doesn't mean that they are heartless people. It doesn't matter what you wear, it doesn't matter what you listen to and it doesn't matter what you look like. It is about your intention; how happy, helpful, and meaningful you want your life to be. It's about how you act and what you think, not what you look like or how you may be perceived. Regardless of the negative labels that our generation may get, most of us have good intentions and we just want to do the best we can with our lives.

Young adults can get a bad rap because it's an age when they are no longer innocent but the maturity of adulthood isn't yet there. You often hear this period of life labeled as "experimental" but I prefer the term "experiential." There are a lot of firsts between the ages of 13-25—it's a long stretch. First kiss, first time driving, and first time living on your own (hopefully), along with so many other "firsts." If we're to get through these unknown "firsts" with a smooth recovery, we need to incorporate our spirituality into every decision. These aren't shallow decisions, at least not if we chose wisely. With age comes privilege but it also comes with tremendous responsibility. It's important that we acknowledge both, rather than just the freedom, because if we're not careful that supposed freedom could entrap us all too quickly in more responsibilities than we may be ready for. We need our beliefs to keep us on our track.

Undeniably, life is rife with temptations and if we don't have that internal compass guiding us, it's easy to get lost. And while some of these choices may seem like quick and easy routes to happiness, they can be all too misleading. It's the disciplined decisions that can be the hardest to make that ultimately lead to our well-being and happiness. If we don't have our spirituality helping us sort through the murky waters of decision making, life can quickly feel as though it's in utter disarray. Here's what some of you shared with me.

Sunny Samples

1.   Julia: "I am tested almost daily in my spirituality. Doubts and fears have a way of sneaking into my mind, causing me great distress and unhappiness. But in the end, I revert to what I know to be true; everything works in God's time for His glory. When I can lay aside those fears and place my troubles in His hands, I am happy with where my life is and where it is going. It is a daily struggle to find that place of peace, and easier said than done. I love being in control, but when I realize that the world is not mine to control, I cease to be unhappy with the way things are. Instead, I feel hopeful for the way they may soon become."

2.   Jay: "On more than one occasion, especially in times of disappointment or unhappiness, I have instinctively questioned my spirituality, and more specifically, my faith in God. This reminds me that by allowing our deepest held beliefs in God to stand up against all questions of uncertainty and doubt, we can go forward in difficult times and still be happy."

3.   Cynthia: "Have I been tested in my spirituality before? Oh yeah... so many times! God seems to always be testing me. Having epilepsy at a young age, I have already faced a lot. I have not only endured brain surgery, but my parents have been less than supportive. They have actually been abusive. I had a very difficult family situation and I have often asked, 'Why God?' 'Why me?' I believe that one day I will find out why He *let me* have the home life I did. I believe everything happens for a reason, and

that everything will be used for His glory. I believe He has been working on making me a stronger, more patient person. All in all, my hardship has strengthened me physically and emotionally and I'm a much happier person with God by my side than if I'd been standing alone."

It's interesting to me how Cynthia said God "let" her have the things that He did. And isn't it true? We are not given anything to have forever—we are merely leant things to either enjoy or make the best of in our lives. I hope you'll see whatever is given to you in your life as a blessing rather than a burden. Instead of asking, "Why is this happening to me?" I challenge you to ask, "How can this experience make me a stronger person?"

There's a particular story I want to share with you. If there is someone who has experienced temptation and conquered it, by the power vested in spirituality, it is Danielle. Danielle was still in high school when she wrote this and it's incredible how much she's endured and still overcame. Here is her story:

> *"Everyone who knows me knows I am in Alcoholics Anonymous (AA). There is a lot of controversy in our community whether or not to remain anonymous to the people we know. I feel like it is a fundamental part of my being I share with all my friends, family, co-workers, and teachers. I feel like not only do people need to know, in case they have a family member who is an alcoholic, or they themselves are an alcoholic, but also so that people know that alcoholics can be 18, they can be girls, and it is not just a bunch of old men. Take the alcohol away and we are still the same people with the same amount of wreckage in our lives. But now we handle that wreckage by becoming spiritually fit and better people.*
>
> *Even in the process of trying to become a better person, I got a lot of bad reactions. I have been turned down from jobs because I am in the program, but honestly, I need a job that is not going to schedule me on Friday nights or Sunday mornings or whenever I have commitments at my meetings. A lot of people judge me, there are a lot of guys who won't date me, or people who have resentments toward me because their family members are alcoholics and they hate all*

alcoholics--recovered or not. I am open about it because I am truly a genuine person who is never going to put on a front like I am perfect, or that I have a perfect family, or a perfect job, or the best life.

I first went to AA when I was 14 after I got alcohol poisoning and a ticket for being drunk in public. I stayed sober for nine months in the program until my parents told me that I could no longer attend AA because they did not like the people I was hanging out with. In reality, my parents are alcoholics and they do not like to see that I am making good friendships or becoming a better person because they are not doing the same. So, on my own, I stayed for another year, but then started taking pills and I eventually started drinking again.

My first spiritual experience was when my mom told me that I should go back to AA, when I called her crying saying that I got invited to drink at my friend's house. Oh, how I wanted to change my life around. That was only part of the miracle...the real miracle happened later that night. It was a Saturday night and I knew where there was a Sunday AA meeting and I couldn't decide if I should go or not. I could not sleep because I was so overwhelmed with fear and anxiety. Right before I went to bed I got on Facebook and I still had four friends from AA. Three of them had started drinking again and only one of them was still sober. I went on Facebook around 4:00 in the morning and the only person who was online was my friend from AA who was still sober. I messaged him and asked him if he would take me to the meeting and he said 'yes.' He told me he would call me in the morning and make sure that I was still going. He even offered to meet me beforehand so I would have someone to go with and feel more comfortable. Honestly, I felt that God intervened. My friend had literally saved me that night. I woke up and he did just what he said he would and I have been sober from that day on. God is faithful.

Another profound experience happened six months ago when I was in San Francisco. I was looking in the area where I had been accepted for college. I was driving with my cousin and she asked me if I was going to attend an AA meeting that night. I told her probably not because I had gone to two meetings the night before and didn't like either of them. But she insisted that I go to a meeting so I pulled over on a side street, parked the car, and called the AA office in San Francisco. This was unusual because I never pull over to make a call. Just then, a lady walking her dog came up to the side of my car and said to my cousin, 'Oh, are you looking for an AA meeting?' I immediately hung up the phone. The lady then proceeded to tell me some good meetings and circled a particular one in the AA directory saying it was an awesome meeting and I MUST go to it. As she departed I watched her walk into her house, which was literally right in front of where I had parked.

Of course I went. As the meeting was about to begin, I started chatting with a woman. She asked me where I was from, and when I told her she said she had family in the same area and that she had been to a few meetings in the area. I asked her which ones and she said she had attended the same 7:00 am meeting that I attend almost every morning—the same place I met my sponsor. I don't know if you understand how rare this is. In my town, there are over one hundred AA meetings a week. The likelihood of someone going to that same meeting, especially when it begins at 7:00 AM is simply amazing.

The whole series of events made me cry tears of joy, which were the first tears of joy I have ever cried in my lifetime. The presence of God was so overwhelming it was crazy. God obviously wanted me to get to an AA meeting."

❋　❋　❋

I don't know about you, but I find this story to be a powerful testimony. Call it coincidence, call it destiny, call it divine intervention—I think it is a testament to how spirituality can offer blessings that lead to tremendous happiness. It's all about perspective.

Sunny Suggestion

Perhaps you believe in miracles, sheer coincidences, or neither. But we can all think back on moments in our life that felt almost magical—perhaps a feeling that was ethereal or not of this world. These are often the moments that can give us a new idea of happiness; we start to see life with new and refreshed eyes. We can't let these "miraculous" moments slip away; we have to capitalize on them if we want to increase our happiness.

Your Sunny Side: What are a few memories you have when your life felt "miraculous" or "magical"?

_____

_____

_____

Your Spiritual Garden

My parents guided me to spirituality. I went to church every week and I said my prayers every night. Faith was like a seed, planted in me at a young age. I like to think that I grew up to be like a sunflower—I have a sunny spirit. But I would be nothing if I didn't have my spirituality strengthening my roots.

I think, in a way, we all embody spiritual flowers. Perhaps you are a pansy; feeling like your spirituality is weak at this time in your life. Maybe you're a poppy, taking spirituality as you need it but closing yourself off when the sun sets. Maybe you're a rose with a seemingly beautiful spirit but you're covered by a few thorny issues that prevent anyone from getting too close to you. We've all got a little bit of every flower variety in us.

Your Sunny Side: If you had to pick a flower that resembled your faith, what would you choose and why?

_____

_____

Like flowers, people can be fragile. How can you strengthen your spirituality?

_____

_____

Here's how some others decided to grow in their spiritual garden.

Sunny Samples

1. Bethany: "I didn't truly find spirituality until I began to debate it with my brother on a philosophical level. He is older than me and he loved to stump me by questioning my faith. Every time this happened, I would spend hours trying to figure out the answer. I finally came up with solutions that reconciled my childhood notions of God. From my life experiences, I looked introspectively and honestly asked myself, 'Do I really believe in God?' I came to the conclusion that if I didn't, what was the purpose of my life? Only by asking those tough questions, and a willingness to question my faith did I finally find my spirituality. I don't believe that God would want us to blindly trust and follow Him. I don't believe that He meant life to be a spectator sport and sure enough, every time I questioned Him or His purpose, I was given an answer. Now, did I always like that answer? No. But it did give me a greater understanding of who He really is. I think this process is necessary, no matter what you decide to believe."

2. Teresa: "My parents were a key part in helping me develop my spirituality. I was raised in a religion where spirituality is essential. My life

has been molded by the values encompassed in this spiritual religion and has allowed me to live a life full of happiness and joy."

3. Kevin: "I think my spirituality, my God, probably found me."

Sunny Suggestion

Know your roots. We need to remember where we came from. If we don't, we might have a hard time understanding how we came to be in the present. No matter where we stand in our beliefs, it's great if we can develop a gratitude for how we developed into our spiritual selves. Whether or not you agree with what your parents believe in, it's important to acknowledge how it may have impacted your life.

Your Sunny Side: How did your family affect your spirituality? How did it affect your happiness?

_____

_____

How has your spirituality developed throughout your life?

_____

_____

Do you feel happier leading a more or less spiritual life and why?

_____

_____

A Teenage Cave of Wonders? Beating Temptation.

At this stage of our growth, there are still so many temptations. These enticements can produce weeds overrunning our spirituality and stifling our happiness. More than ever, we need some extra ladybugs to protect us. But if there is anything that I've learned in my research of this chapter, it's that many young adults are strong in their spirituality.

I was under the impression that this was a time of great testing and trial, with our spirituality struggling to be strong at times. At least, this was the case for me. It wasn't that I stopped believing or that I didn't have faith, it was just that I didn't know how to incorporate my lifelong spirituality into a completely new world of unknown experiences in college. I eventually grew in my faith but it's still a daily challenge to adapt to new circumstances. Our situations in life are ebbing and flowing but it's important that we try to keep our spirituality strong.

Even when I'm feeling overwhelmed, knowing that my spirituality is supporting me reminds me that I can endure. When I am weak, my God is strong. Knowing that you have strength in your spirit can be one of the most empowering yet humbling experiences and it will always carry you through. Here's what you had to say about life's temptations and how your spirituality intervened.

Sunny Samples

1.   Jennifer: "It is definitely easier to be spiritual as a child than as a teenager or an adult. When you are a kid, things are black and white. Stealing is wrong. Lying is wrong. God is in heaven. But as you begin to grow up, you pay attention to the motivations behind actions, and the lines are blurred. Is it really wrong for a father to pick fruit off of a tree, not belonging to him, in order to feed his family? Where do 'white lies' come into play, and is it wrong to lie in order to spare someone's feelings? How can God truly exist, if we can't see Him directly or explain the difference between science and the Bible? Spirituality takes on a whole new face when it comes to ethical questions, and it is much easier to be young and not

have to think so hard about right and wrong. When we can accept without questioning, it is far easier to have faith. But as we grow and learn, we have to reconcile our beliefs with the reality of the world around us, which is in no way a bad thing, but certainly becomes more difficult."

2. David: "I am honestly seeing an increase in spirituality in college. It's like people are thinking: 'There's something out there that I know is there, but cannot identify, and it feels like it might be very important.' It makes people curious. People explore it in different ways. Some go to church, to find that 'something.' That being said, there are also many college students who are throwing morality out the window. Their spirituality is to serve their own needs. They don't want to be told 'don't drink alcohol, don't smoke pot, and don't have sex' because they're thinking, 'Hey, it's fun, and everybody else does it, so why shouldn't I?' So, being moral and spiritual can be extremely difficult in college."

3. Nick: "I think it is easier to follow God as a teenager rather than as a child or adult. As a child your religion is predominately shaped by what your parents believe, and you may not believe what they do. As an adult there are so many responsibilities such as a job, family, and financial security. Many of these material things keep us tied more to the physical world than the spiritual world. The perfect time to develop your own belief system is during your teenage years. You no longer have to believe only what your parents believe and you are not yet tied down to the things of this world."

Sunny Suggestions

1. Let your spirit guide you. When you're young there are so many temptations facing you. And I'm not just talking about drinking or drugs. It can be tempting to stay in a comfortable but stagnant relationship. It can be tempting to accept a good job, instead of holding out a little longer for the great one. It can be tempting to play it safe instead of taking those healthy risks we talked about earlier. But when you let your spirit guide you, you'll have a much better sense of what you should be accepting or letting go of in your life. Listening to your heart will not only help you in your future, but also in your happiness.

Your Sunny Side: What temptations have you encountered recently and how did it affect your happiness?

_____

_____

_____

Did your spirituality, in any way, guide you in your decision-making process? Please explain.

_____

_____

_____

2.   Don't make excuses. I'll admit that I was the first to use the teenage crutch. "Oh, I'm young. This is the time when mistakes are allowed." That lasted for about five minutes when I quickly learned that mistakes, at least intentional ones, are never acceptable. Even though you may think this is the time to try drinking, sex, or whatever else fancies you on a whim, unless it is done in a safe environment, chances are likely that it will end as a mistake. We have to use our spirituality to keep us secure in our values when we are tempted to succumb to peer pressure. There is no better rock in your life than your own strong spirit. You'll also be so much happier when you're guided by your spirituality rather than society's temptations.

Your Sunny Side: Do you think young adults are tempted more than other age groups? How do you think we can overcome these trials to lead happier lives?

_____

_____

For our quote this chapter, I thought I'd share one of my favorites from the Nobel Peace Prize Winner, Mother Teresa:

> **"Life is an opportunity, benefit from it.**
> **Life is beauty, admire it.**
> **Life is a dream, realize it.**
> **Life is a challenge, meet it.**
> **Life is a duty, complete it.**
> **Life is a game, play it.**
> **Life is a promise, fulfill it.**
> **Life is sorrow, overcome it.**
> **Life is a song, sing it.**
> **Life is a struggle, accept it.**
> **Life is a tragedy, confront it.**
> **Life is an adventure, dare it.**
> **Life is luck, make it.**
> **Life is too precious, do not destroy it.**
> **Life is life, fight for it."**

Knowing who you are—having a spiritual strength in your beliefs and values—is an extremely grounding feeling that will give you the confidence you need to be a dedicated, respectable, and happy person. I hope you are willing to allow time for getting to know yourself and what you stand for because when you invest in your spirituality, you are investing in your happiness.

Take Time to
Time Out

Remember how we used to have to take time-outs when you were a toddler in trouble? Well, now it's time to start seeing time-outs as a good thing. If we're ever going to feel content with our lives, we need to take a breath every now and then to step back and simply enjoy the moment. I'm not saying you should sit in a corner by yourself, but I am encouraging you to take some time for yourself that is just for you. It's essential that you allow yourself the opportunity to be at peace with who you are—and the best way to do that is simply by taking the time to find out who you are and what will make you happy.

Our attitudes and beliefs change throughout our lives but we all have a fundamental core identity no matter where we are, whom we're with, or what we're doing. People can have different personalities for different occasions, but ultimately, you know who you are. And even with so many external life changes, no matter how old we are, we still want the same things throughout life: safety, peace, love and happiness.

Treasure Your Time Alone

Although it's a beautiful thing to surround yourself with the people you love, you still need a healthy balance of time alone. This time for yourself doesn't have to mean social isolation. As much as we may be social creatures, we need time to rejuvenate and give ourselves a mental check-up on how we're feeling. We need to allow ourselves enough time to process what's going on in our lives or it could quickly pass us by. We need to process the lessons we're learning. Don't do a cram session on your life—allow yourself time for it all to sink in. Here's what many of you shared with me when it came to time for yourself.

Sunny Samples

1.   Sydney: "Being alone is like being on vacation. Every few days it's refreshing to just take time off to think. I sit by myself in almost silence. I mark things off my mental 'to-do' list and straighten out my feelings about the days' happenings. My happiness comes from being sure of myself and knowing the 'whys' of what I do. I can accomplish this best in my alone time."

2.   Dani: "When I'm alone I feel like I'm being recharged... like my battery has been out of juice and is finally getting plugged back into my main source. I NEED time to myself or I feel frustrated and off-kilter."

3.   Jason: "I like being alone sometimes but when I don't want to be alone and I'm forced to be alone, it can drive me CRAZY."

4.   Stacy: "In my free time, I love to read. It's so cool to immerse yourself in a whole different reality when you read, but at the same time you still get to use your imagination in a way that you can't when you watch movies. It makes me so happy when I come across a book that I think is absolutely brilliant."

5.   Libby: "My feelings about being alone vary from time to time. When there's something really difficult going on in my life, like a break up or some other really big change, being alone feels like the worst thing in the world. I need people around for support. But when things are going well, being alone is incredibly rewarding. Don't get me wrong, I love spending time with people, but getting to be by myself for a while each day is key to my happiness. It helps me reset and get ready for tomorrow. It is SO nice to sit in my room and say, 'What am I going to do right now?' and not have the answer depend on anyone other than myself. This might sound silly,

108

but it is honestly so much fun to just dance around to a catchy song in my jammies, singing and looking like an idiot sometimes. I always feel really refreshed after a morning, afternoon, or evening alone at home."

Some of us like our time alone more than others but, as with all things, it's about balance. Alone time can be great—if you're smart about it. Once you start getting bogged down by boredom, then being alone can feel like a death sentence. If anyone gets cabin fever, it's me. There's nothing I dislike more than feeling stir crazy sitting at home fumbling for things to do. Alone time that turns into loneliness can have dire consequences. According to Bearman and Moody in 2004 and Shaffer in 1987, social isolation has been linked to drug and alcohol abuse, lowered immune function, higher rates of cancer and even a higher risk for mortality. Spending time alone is a stressful situation if we don't handle it wisely. But if you choose to do something meaningful with your "me-moments," as I like to call them, then alone time can be a very gratifying experience. So what do I do with my "me-moments?"

In my spare time, I love to write. It feels mindlessly freeing when I get lost in the words and it gives me greater insight into my thoughts. I sometimes struggle to start writing because there is an element of losing control that I battle with in my head, but ultimately, once I let my ideas free, there is no stopping me. My fingers become like my legs, never wanting to stop running on my keyboard. I love the sound of the unsteady rhythm between free-flowing thoughts and moments of deliberation. My fingers dancing on my desktop becomes a chant, a mantra in my mind and I go to another world where the concepts of my subconscious suddenly become conscious on my computer screen. I love when I'm able to let go and just write.

I'm also a huge advocate of downward dogging—that's yoga for those of you who haven't been exposed to the power of the mat. Yoga is such a therapeutic process for my soul and my spine. (I have scoliosis and my spine curves like a snake so staying flexible is very important to me). Also, I love to reconnect with my spirituality through yoga. It's all about getting in touch with your mind, body and soul and if you can settle down enough to sit still for a while, it can really work. And hey, if my 55-year-old dad can become a world-class yogi (he took more than 100 classes in 2011 as a New Year's resolution), then I highly suggest you give sun salutations a shot.

I also love long, luxurious bubble baths. Thank you, Gracie Lou Freebush. (All you *Miss Congeniality* lovers will know what I'm talking about. I did compete in a few pageants after all).

If you are creative and content with your free time, having time alone can provide some of your happiest and most inspired moments. Here are some suggestions for making the most of your free time.

Sunny Suggestions

1. Come up with a rainy day list: I love ongoing lists that you can add to whenever your creativity is sparked. Try to come up with a mini Sunny Set for the days when you feel like you have nothing to do. (Those days may be few and far between but take advantage of any free time you're given—it's a gift). It's often when we're bored that we get that brain block, so having that list prepared ahead of time will give you some automatic ideas to make your time more meaningful.

Your Sunny Side: What are five things you can do when you feel like you have nothing to do that will make you happy?

1. _____

2. _____

3. _____

4. _____

5. _____

2. Pick up some peaceful habits. We could all use a little more relaxation in our lives. Perhaps you are a natural peace lover but if not, I suggest finding some activities that will help you settle down. Things like yoga, writing in a journal or even baking can be great ways to invest in your contentment and overall happiness.

Your Sunny Side: What are some things you could start up to help you wind down?

_____

_____

3. Make the time. Sometimes our days can become so stressful that before we know it, we're already in bed preparing for the next day. With your new habit of writing to-do lists, integrate time for yourself each day. It's just as important as mailing that check or writing that essay. If you don't invest in yourself, you won't be nearly as productive or helpful. Not to mention that your happiness will start to be hindered. You are always worth it. Don't ever forget that.

Your Sunny Side: When would be a good time to have your "me-moment" in the day and what can you do to make sure you have a little time each day just to relax?

_____

_____

Getting Wasted Wastes Your Happiness

We all need to take chill pills every now and then. Now, that does not mean Adderall or Xanax for all you sleep deprived, study-crazed students. Which brings me to the question, why do so many smart students feel the need to "get stupid" (thanks to Mac Dre for that expression) when it comes to 'taking care of' their stress? Because popping pills, doing drugs, or excessively drinking is *stupid* (sorry for my lack of a better word), especially when it's used as a method to de-stress. Perhaps some do it because they think it will give us a momentary breath of happiness, but as many have found, a happiness "high" is often short-lived and quickly replaced by additional stress, embarrassment, or potentially something worse.

You may be wondering why I choose to address this issue in the "Time for Yourself" chapter instead of something like the health chapter. Well, my answer is that many young adults see drinking, smoking, and the like as a "time for themselves" when they can let go of the stress of school, work, and everything in between. But spending our time off in this way will only push us farther from our happiness and our goals. It's important to address this issue because as happiness boosters, drinking and drugs can be deceiving—they are actually depressants and some of the greatest threats to our joy.

I'm going to keep it straight and simple. Not only are drinking and drugs bad for your physical health, they're bad for your emotional health. The problem is that some young adults get trapped in a mirage of what appears to be carefree fun and a good time. When they anticipate a night out, they can't always see what's coming at the end of the night; like a toilet bowl or waking up somewhere where they shouldn't be. You don't necessarily plan these things when you're primping in front of the mirror but if you don't make good decisions, you can quickly find yourself in some pretty humiliating or even dangerous situations. Even small, seemingly inconsequential choices can lead to insurmountable consequences if you're not careful. And I guarantee that you won't feel too happy or proud of yourself when you've put yourself, your friends and family in a position you all don't want to be in.

I don't mean for a second to sound degrading—that is certainly not my intention. If anything, I want to help our generation make the right decisions before we fall down—literally and figuratively speaking. Sure, when you're 21, social drinking can be fun if done responsibly and in moderation—but I've seen too many broken bones, too many sick nights, and too many fatal car accidents, like my uncle's, to stay silent. I know what it's like to watch someone make one bad decision that can lead to a lifetime of tragedy. I know what it's like when someone makes just one wrong choice and then their life is simply over. It's more than just our happiness; it's about protecting our safety and the safety of others. This is an issue that is very important to me and I will always stand up for making smart, safe choices. I hope you will too.

I feel as strongly as I do because of my family history. My parents have each lost their brother (my two uncles) to alcohol related events. One of them I never even met. He was driving under the influence and drove straight into a brick wall. Just like that, an intelligent, promising 24 year old—gone by 2:00 am in the morning. I wish I could have met him but instead I only know him through family photos and a few stories. My other uncle I knew quite well. I watched him go through his battle with alcoholism for over ten years. Seeing that changed my life. It is one of those experiences that words cannot describe but you know you will never be the same. It is because of these two men that I take a step back and reflect—how do I really I want to spend my time? How do I really want to live my life? Whether it's one simple mistake or a lifetime of bad decisions, I've learned that you don't always get second chances. I know that if I'm going to be happy, I can't make those same mistakes. Here's what some of you had to say about it.

Sunny Samples

1. Tori: "I don't do drugs so I don't know how those might affect my happiness, but I do know that alcohol tends to bring me down. I just notice that when I don't drink alcohol for a few weeks, I feel happier. I'm happy when I'm sober even if I don't have something super exciting and entertaining going on."

2. Holly: "For me, alcohol and drugs are the enemy of happiness. Obviously they affect the brain so actions and decisions are usually bad ones. I would say in my experience of drinking and watching others drink, 9 out of 10 times people regret something they did the night before. I, as well as a classmate, have been to the hospital because of alcohol. It is a sad, scary situation and it can cause a deep depression. I am lucky to have

learned from my past mistakes. I have forgiven myself and I now realize alcohol will never make me, or anyone else, happy. Those who say they 'self-medicate' with alcohol would be safer playing with matches. Drinking alcohol is a ticking time bomb for depression."

3. Brian: "Of course drinking can make people happy. I do not see anything wrong with having a good time as long as people are safe and not harming others. Unfortunately, harming others often happens with alcohol consumption. My sister was drunk and she was nearly killed by a driver who did not see her skipping ahead in a crosswalk. This showed me how easily a precious life can be taken from us. We are only given one life and we need to respect others and protect ourselves."

4. Taylor: "I am not a big partier, but I do like to go out with friends every so often. I am not big on drinking, even though I do so on some occasions. Alcohol can make us lose control. I like being in control of my body and for that matter, my life."

5. Jessica: "After turning 21 and having some beers or shots of drinks with friends, I can say that I enjoy alcohol in moderation. I wouldn't go so far as to say that it makes me happier, but I like the social side of drinking with friends and letting loose a little...so I'd say to some extent, alcohol helps provide a happy atmosphere."

No matter what your stance, standing up for yourself is more important than joining in if you don't feel comfortable. I hope that you can have the courage and confidence to decide what is best for you and the people that you are with. I believe that you are smart, strong, and stable. Being safe will lead to not only your happiness today, but also for the morning after when you're not battling a nasty hangover.

Your Sunny Side: If you're put in a situation that could be harmful to yourself or others, what can you do to make the right decision?

_____

_____

How does drinking affect your happiness?

_____

_____

Zuckerberg, You are NOT Helping Me Get in My Zen

I'll admit that probably like some of you, my alone time is not always time well spent. I think I keep Facebook in business both when I have nothing better to do and even when I have something better to do. What an epic waste of time, right?! All I get after a Facebook and reality TV rendezvous is wasted time, and often an unintentional 300 calories afterwards to seal the deal. I certainly don't feel happier afterward. So what can we do to *actually* relax and lead happier lives, besides looking at Facebook profiles from people you've met only once? It might seem a bit of an oxymoron, but if we want to relax we have to do so actively. Spending our time by just sitting and staring at a screen may shut down our minds, but it won't turn up our happiness level. It's a conscious choice. Here's what some of you do to relax—and it doesn't include zoning out on Facebook or another episode of the Kardashians.

Sunny Samples

1.   Sarah: "I find any activity that's more physical than mental to be really relaxing. Coming home and doing chores like washing the dishes and folding the laundry is therapeutic because it lets my mind quiet down after a long day. Also, when I have time, I love hiking. The fresh air and the scenery are both so relaxing."
2.   Sydney: "I relax by taking a shower, shaving my legs, and wearing a big, long sleep shirt. Then, I love to sit in my bed and write or draw in my journal, play The Sims, or read a book. Sometimes I like to just start cooking in the kitchen without a recipe. My recipe creation gives me much happiness! My happiness level increases if it's just me at home."

3. Jesse: "I relax by listening to music, playing the piano, or sleeping. When I'm relaxed and I'm in my own world, nothing else matters. I'm happy."

Sunny Suggestion

Take the time. I hope you'll take time, every now and then, to just sit with yourself and enjoy your own company. It doesn't have to last forever and you don't have to instigate a start and stop time—just do what feels right for you. We all need our own space to become our own person.

Your Sunny Side: When you're alone, what do you do to relax?

_____

_____

What can you do to add to your "relax routine?"

_____

_____

Many of you treasure your time alone and some of you are always itching to be surrounded by others. It depends on what you're used to. As for me, I've been on both sides of the fence. Growing up, I treasured my Saturday morning date of Barbie, Ken, and myself. Mind you this was when I was seven, not seventeen. But now that I've experienced college, I am quick to get lonely after a day apart from my friends. I miss the constant laughter and I love having someone to talk to about the miniscule and the meaningful parts of the day. But no matter where you are, people adapt to the living situation they're familiar with, whether they're alone in a one room flat or they're in the crowded hall of a college dorm (gotta love those communal bathrooms...not), and we can all find happiness no matter where we live if we're willing to look hard enough. There is an adjustment period but eventually you can find something to appreciate about your circumstances.

Sunny Suggestions

1. **Realize what there is to love.** You can't always control where you live, but you can control your view of the situation. No matter where you are, there is something to be grateful for. Perhaps your best friend lives right next door or you love the university you go to. Change may not be easy, but the sooner you learn to accept it, the sooner you can be happy.

Your Sunny Side: What is there to love about where you live?

_____

_____

2. **Be with the people who matter.** Find those friends who will make you happy, no matter where you are. It's like the song by Edward Sharpe and the Magnetic Zeros: "Home is whenever I'm with you." So whether you're at home, or home is one thousand miles away, spend time with the people who will make you feel like you can relax, even if it's via Skype.

Your Sunny Side: Who are some of the people in your life who put you at ease?

_____

_____

3. **Create a place of peace.** No matter where you are, if you try, you can always find just a few minutes for yourself. If that time doesn't come naturally when you need it most, it's fair to excuse yourself and let others

know that you just need a little time to think and be with our own thoughts. Otherwise the thoughts of others could too quickly become our own.

Your Sunny Side: Even when it gets hectic, what can you do to create time for yourself?

_____

_____

Caring Enough to Comprehend

No matter where we are, or who we're surrounded by, it's crucial that we take our alone time when we need it. We should sit with our thoughts and listen to what our heart is telling us. Give yourself an opportunity to reflect and gain perspective on your situation. When I have time to myself, I like to think about what I really want for my life. Here's what some of you thought about in your free time.

Sunny Samples

1. James: "I reflect on my life during my alone time and sometimes I think too much! I question if I'm truly happy with where I am but I also get frustrated when I don't know what I want. I struggle a lot with regret when I think about my life. In order for my happiness not to be negatively affected, I have a 'calm down' routine where I settle in my hopefulness even if I don't know where my life will take me."
2. Tyler: "Thinking can sometimes bring me down because I'm not happy with some of the choices I've made and I know I need to fix them."
3. Sophie: "I think all the time, especially before I go to sleep. Sometimes it makes me happy, sometimes nostalgic, sometimes motivated, and sometimes remorseful! It depends on what I'm thinking about."

As easy as it can be to base our self-worth on what we have or have not accomplished, it's so important that we have gratitude and humbleness when we have time to reflect. Life isn't about names—what brand of clothes you wear, what school you go to, or where you work. Life is about leaving a positive legacy and being a person that you are proud to be. When we look back and when we look ahead, we shouldn't base our happiness on how much money we've made or what titles we've received, we should get our happiness from being good to ourselves and generous to others. The happiest people are those who are compassionate, loyal, and loving.

You can go to sleep at night knowing that in your heart, you always try to do the right thing. When you make your decisions out of love for others and respect for yourself, you won't have to convince yourself to be happy. It will come naturally to you. It's the gift you receive for giving your best to the world.

Of course we will make mistakes that can threaten our happiness. Admit them. Forgive those who have hurt you. Be at peace in your heart and find balance in your life. This will bring you the happiness you desire. Here are some Sunny Suggestions to inspire your well-being.

Sunny Suggestions

1. **Keep a journal**. A journal is one of the best gifts you can give yourself. You can tell it things that you can't tell anyone else—your deepest dreams, most frustrating challenges, and yes, even your romances that seem just as perplexing at 21 as they did when you were 13.

I love journals for two reasons. The first is that they help you remember. Call me crazy, but the first one-hundred days of my first serious relationship, I noted what happened in our relationship—every day. I wrote down every movie we saw, every outing we went on, and so on. It might seem a little odd, but I'm so glad that I did this because I remembered so much more of our relationship and in turn, our time together was all the more meaningful. You'd be surprised at how easy it is to forget all the dinner dates and the special occasions if you don't make note of them. What may have seemed like one of the best days of your life can feel like a distant memory if you don't make note of it.

The second reason I love journaling is because it reminds us of who we really are. Personally, I'm amazed to see how similar I am throughout the years. It's made me a firm believer in our core identity. Even when I think I've changed so much—become so worldly and intellectual at the old age of 21 (just kidding!)—in so many ways, I'm really just the same girl that I was when I was 10 years old. I've always had goals for myself, I've always loved to write, and I've always loved looking in to my relationships—no matter what my age. Writing in your journal keeps the journey alive. Otherwise, unlike the ink on the page, our memories and goals fade with time.

Furthermore, history can repeat itself if we're not careful. When we're about to make the same mistake twice, the pages in our journal can give us the perfect information when we need to get our lives back on track. A journal can be one of the most valuable learning devices. Yet as helpful as they are, I found that many young adults don't have journals, and for those who do, many often start only the first few pages before it just collects dust in the back of a drawer. But for those of you who do keep a journal, here's what you had to say.

Sunny Samples

1. Myha: "I keep a journal and when I have a really great day, I write it down. Memories are important to me and I like to be reminded of those days. I remember how really happy I was, and when I re-read it, it makes me happy all over again."

2. Jordan: "I don't write in my journal every night, but I write when I need to let feelings out--whether they're really good or bad. Writing affects my happiness in a positive way. I don't feel relieved or as though a huge weight has been lifted… I just simply feel better. It also gives me so much happiness to read my entries from the week before or even a year before; those are the most fun!"

3. Danielle: "I keep a journal (but not a traditional one) that I use daily. It is full of quotes, whether they are from unknown people I hear on the street that day or ones I read about...or quotes from my beloved books. I also include my favorite Latin phrases and Bible verses."

I encourage you to give journaling a go. You might find that you actually really enjoy it. You don't have to pressure yourself to write daily—just write when you feel compelled. You'll know when the time is right to write.

Your Sunny Side: Do you keep a journal? If so, how does it affect your happiness? If not, how do you think journaling could help you during your time for yourself?

_____

_____

2. Keep a blog. Journals don't have to be your only outlet. I'm also an advocate for online journals, your very own blog—private or public. Blogs are a great way to invest in yourself while still connecting with others. I have kept a blog for over three years and I've loved every minute of it. It is much more interactive than a journal. People can share, comment, or even write their own entries on your blog. For me, it's like an online scrapbook filled with pictures, meaningful stories, and special people that have contributed to and changed my life for the better. Blogging is a quick and easy community journal that allows many people to share and participate.

Sunny Sample

1. Kelsey: "I don't keep a journal, but I do have a blog that I've been writing since 2006. Blogging is great because it's like having a journal you can share with your friends. Any form of journal writing is great because it allows you to hold on to happy memories, while also giving you a kind of loyal listener for when you're having problems. People constantly change and, if nothing else, I think it's really interesting that I can read back through my blog and see who I was when I was 15, 16, 17, and now, 18, and read about the events that have most impacted my life."

A word of caution though, be sure to respect the privacy of others. My personal life includes many other people's personal lives and just because I feel comfortable sharing my life stories on the internet doesn't mean that I have the right to share the lives of others as well. You certainly have to write with discretion (or at least that's what I highly recommend) so that, along with your own, you can hold on to your family and friends' privacy.

Your Sunny Side: What are you inspired to write about?

_____

_____

I guarantee you'll feel happier when you've settled down enough to sit and reflect on your thoughts. When you allow yourself to delve into the creative energy of your goals and you remind yourself of your passion for certain pursuits, you will certainly feel more content with who you are. Don't let yourself forget that you are going places and that you will eventually get there! Here's this chapter's quote:

"But what is happiness except the simple harmony between a man and the life he leads?" –Albert Camus

When you can find peace with who you are and the way you live your life, you can be truly happy. Taking time for yourself is essential if you are going to know yourself and what you will and won't stand for. Take a stance. Have an idea. Start a fire within yourself. Take the time you have for yourself and use it wisely. Show up for a meeting with yourself and get to know who you are and what you love about life. If there's anybody worth meeting, it's you.

Sunny
Socials

Let's kick off with **Your Sunny Side** right off the bat. What does *your* perfect day look like?

_____

_____

_____

_____

Maybe you wrote something along the lines of a day spent with your best friend, your mom, or by yourself. Or a day playing your favorite sport, buying the perfect outfit, or cuddling with your pet. Or maybe a day relaxing—not doing much, or one that is full of activities with things to do and places to be. I'll bet it's a little bit of everything. Now on to the next question.

Do you feel like you live your perfect day most days? What are your days often like?

_____

_____

_____

And now the homerun question, are you happy on most days? Why or why not?

_____

_____

_____

No matter how happy you are with your life right now, I hope that *your* perfect day can be every day. I hope it can include watching a great film, taking a walk on the beach, or sharing an amazing kiss. The key concept is that perfect is still imperfect. Perfection really only comes in those spontaneous, beautiful moments in our life that we can simply enjoy without any pressure. Besides, when we're trying so hard for perfection, it is often anything but. In fact perfection can quickly lead to procrastination.

Our perfect day doesn't have to be perfect in the way we might imagine: like a trip to Hawaii or Ryan Reynolds romancing us. If life is going to be anything close to perfect, we have to get real with ourselves. You can be realistically happy if you can realize that perfect is an idea we need to put in perspective. So let me ask again, in case you got a little swept up the first time.

Realistically, what does your perfect day look like?

_____

_____

_____

_____

_____

In case you need some ideas, here's what some of you do on your perfect days.

Sunny Samples

1. Alex: "I think my perfect day would start with a breakfast of delicious waffles. I would then go to the park with my family and have a huge picnic and party. The day would come to an end by playing a water polo game with my friends, and having a sleepover where we stayed up all night."

2. Ben: "My perfect day is having friends around me, doing all the things I want without being tired, going somewhere adventurous, eating something delicious, meeting someone fantastic, and living in the present."

3. Emily: "A really good morning run and hanging out with friends all day."

4. Wes: "My perfect day would be waking up at 5:00 in the morning and taking the boat to the lake with my good friends and spending all day on the water swimming, tubing, wakeboarding, and just having fun."

5. Kimberly: "I love a day that is completely spontaneous. There is no real order to what we do or where we go. My only requirement is being surrounded by my family if I am home and by my close friends if I am at school. It's the people that make my day. I try to surround myself with positive people."

My perfect day is one where I feel like I have made a contribution, both to myself and to someone else. I love having at least one (and maybe just one) delicious meal (the last time I attempted two buffets in one day I barely made it). There needs to be a lot of laughter that comes *from people* and not just the TV (sorry, but watching "The Office" just doesn't cut it). I also love a good cuddle with my Siamese cat and a heartfelt talk with my best friends. I wouldn't mind a perfect day that includes a fantastic kiss, meaningful conversations, and a little time laying in the sun (hey, Vitamin D is bound to boost your happiness a bit!). A perfect day also has writing that is fulfilling rather than fumbling, singing that sounds mildly decent—and doing a little shopping doesn't hurt either. Oh and a good book? Done. It's already a great day. But actually, if I did just one of these things, it makes for a perfect day. Every day is just a little bit perfect if I take the time to put a little joy in everything I do and everywhere I go. If I can go to sleep at night knowing that I made one friendship stronger, myself healthier, or one person happier, then it is perfect in my eyes.

It is the joy and passion we put in to our life that truly creates a perfect day. Whether we are passionate about a certain hobby or the people who participate with us, we are taking a step in the right direction when we dedicate our efforts towards what makes us happy. Life can be so fulfilling if we follow our heart and then lead with our mind. I wanted to know when you wake up in the morning, what it is that makes you *naturally* happy.

Sunny Samples

1. William: "I am passionate about volleyball. Volleyball is my way of taking a break from real life. It's my happy place. It influences my happiness because it's something that allows me to be myself, be competitive, explore my weaknesses and strengths, surround myself with good people, and exercise while having fun."

2. Kimber: "During my first year in college I discovered a passion for studying gerontology. I know it sounds strange but I love the study of aging. Through the study of gerontology I came into contact with residents of a retirement home. I found my conversations with them to be insightful and refreshing. Being able to set aside time to visit with them, especially when things at school get hectic, is key for me. It keeps things in perspective. I am not discrediting the relationships I have with those my age, but older generations have wisdom that is truly priceless. They see the bigger picture, and their insight is something that often helps me make sense of the hard times while treasuring the good times."

3.   Adam: "I am passionate about creativity. Just being able to create, or helping someone else create, whether it is a new way to make coffee at work or it's making movies, I am always passionate about new ideas and new creations."

4.   Heather: "I'm definitely passionate about all music. I also recently discovered my passion for literature. I wish I would have discovered this passion in high school because it would have helped out quite a bit, but I'm just so glad I've found it now. I'm not sure exactly how it influences my happiness, but the fact that words can influence my emotions so much, whether it is happy or sad, lets me know that loving books so much has to have a positive effect on my life somehow."

5.   Avery: "When I was little, I felt my passions were things like swimming and reading. As I grow older, I find my passions consist of things like helping those less fortunate and those with special needs. My nephew has autism, and I realized that every time I get involved myself in one of his activities, whether it was the Special Olympics or the Autism Walk, I felt overwhelmed with joy and gratefulness. The more I help others, the happier I feel; both sides benefit from the gift of giving."

Don't Ever Pass on the Passion

Passion is essential in order to lead a fulfilling, happy life. My passions throughout life have given me something to look forward to and have also given me an exponential amount of happiness. There's no better feeling than setting out to study or practice a new skill and finding that it brings you so much happiness. You lose track of time and your mind becomes stable and focused. *You're in the moment.*

Even though I may no longer continue with different hobbies that I've tried throughout my life, the experiences gained and the lessons learned are never in vain. Whether it was gymnastics as a little girl or student leadership in high school, those experiences will always be a part of me and they make me who I am today. The skills you acquire throughout life will carry you on and continually add to your happiness in one way or another. Here's how you can increase your happiness by following your interests.

Sunny Suggestions

1.   Take a walk down memory lane. When you're young, the answers are much more simple—you did what you liked to do. You were interested in soccer, so you played. You wanted to try out ballet, so you danced. As we get older, life can start to hold us back due to our fear, potential embarrassment, or a lack of time or money—the setbacks are endless. But rekindling that old flame that made you come alive when you were young is a good thing to bring back into your life. Put a new spin on what used to make you happy; chances are, it still will.

Your Sunny Side: What were some activities, school subjects, or hobbies that you loved pursuing when you were young?

_____

_____

How can you incorporate these passions into your life now?

_____

_____

2.   Bring a friend. Sometimes the biggest thing holding us back from our happiness is that we're either afraid of looking like a fool learning something new or that we'll feel lonely in the process. Chances are, you have a friend who is interested in similar activities, so bring a buddy along when you're trying something new. Maybe you've both wanted to learn how to surf or you wish you knew another language. Having a friend along can be a huge source of encouragement and motivation—not to mention that you'll add to each other's happiness by helping each other.

Your Sunny Side: What are some new activities you'd like to try and which friends would you like to bring along?

1. _____

2. _____

3. _____

3.   Be brave. We all have dreams. Who says they can't become a reality? Just because it's a dream doesn't mean it can't come true. Maybe you've always wanted to learn to play the piano or you wished you were on your high school tennis team. It's never too late. Sometimes a new challenge can offer us the most happiness so don't be afraid to explore.

Your Sunny Side: What are three new activities that you want to try out and how can you start?

1. _____

2. _____

3. _____

It's important to be proud of our passions. Society often encourages us to diminish our successes and hold back our enthusiasm when we achieve. You deserve to celebrate, especially when you've really worked hard. Acing that test that you diligently studied for or landing that jump that you've been practicing for the past two months can undoubtedly make you happy. Don't be afraid to share the happiness of success with others. We have to capitalize on those moments because it is a reminder that anything is possible if we are willing to put in the work.

At the same time, it's just as important to be humble. One thing my boyfriend (who is the most humble person I know) told me was how arrogance is a person's greatest downfall. I couldn't agree more. It's that moment where subtle confidence turns into loud cockiness. The respect people have for you turns into rejection the moment you decide you're better than everyone else. So again, I bring up the word balance. While it's important to make note of what you've earned and celebrate it, if you want to lead a happy life, it's just as important to stay humble. It's a balance that many of the most successful people in the world maintain; they are sure of the skills they possess, but they don't need to shout it out to stand out.

I was curious what my fellow authors were most proud of in their lives. It wasn't always an award or a medal. They're more proud of their relationships, their hard work, and their character. Medals get tarnished, trophies get dusty, but the satisfaction of a job well done never gets old.

Sunny Samples

1.   Katie: "My proudest accomplishment has been excelling academically. I am so proud that I go to one of the top universities in the nation, and that I get to take classes taught by accomplished professors who inspire me every day to dream big. This has affected my happiness in a very positive way because it has given me a sense of accomplishment. I believe that happiness is not only defined by what things we have in our lives, but also by what we do and what we achieve."

2.   Greg: "I'm proud of my relationship with my parents. I have always been close to my parents but now that I am getting older, I have really strengthened my relationship with them."

3.   Nick: "I have two achievements that I am equally proud of. I reached the rank of Eagle Scout and I won a state championship in volleyball. I was

a boy scout for 12 years and throughout those 12 years I grew into a man. Setting a goal for myself that took 12 years to accomplish isn't an easy task for anyone. Knowing this, I am proud of myself for completing all of the requirements and passing all of the tests to become an Eagle Scout. It was also a fun experience. I met a lot of my good friends and I had amazing memories while on the trail and out in the wild. I got to explore whatever my heart desired and I really had a chance to find myself.

Now, winning a state championship in a sport that truly has taken over my life was an unbelievable moment. I've been playing volleyball for only six years, and in those six years, besides school, volleyball has become the biggest part of my life. I never imagined being part of a team that would make it to a championship. But throughout the season we started to flourish and bond. We really got close and started believing that we had a real shot at the championship. It was amazing to watch our team progress into what we became at the end of the season. I am grateful for the experience and will never forget the time we spent on the top of the state leader board."

4.   Grace: "My proudest accomplishment could be a lot of things, but I am one who prefers not to 'rest on their laurels.' Therefore, while I have been blessed with talents and abilities that have brought me success, I think that being a big sister for my younger sister and brother is truly my proudest accomplishment. It may seem petty, but at some point in my life I realized that they look up to me. Now that they are in high school and I am away, I see what an important influence I have been in their lives. When they make the right choices in life I smile and recall some childhood memory where I know played a part in that choice."

My Sunny Side

When I look back on my life thus far, I'm proud of my fearlessness. You see, even though it may not have been exactly fashionably appropriate, I love that I wore a dress to school every day until sixth grade. I love that I ran for student body president in the eighth grade even though I wasn't the most popular girl in school (I remember my slogan: "Summer, Winter,

Rain or Shine, Lauren Cook is Cooking Up Ideas All the Time!") I love that I sang "I Will Always Love You" in the high school talent show even though I'm no Whitney Houston. And I love that I'm writing this book.

The reason why I love all of these sometimes awkward, yet socially brave moments of my life is because they are the risks that have defined me. Often unbeknownst to me at the time of my risks, I was pulled up from many of life's pitfalls. I wore dresses simply because I liked them—even if other kids would tease me for it. I could have cared less. I ran for student government because I wanted to make a difference. I still do. I sang in the talent show because I love to sing—so why not? I like the thrill that comes from overcoming fears.

Overall, I'm not afraid to say it, I'm not afraid to wear it, I'm not afraid to campaign for it, and I'm not afraid to walk away. Choices like these, where I look back and even think, "What the heck was I thinking?"—I then go on to think, "I was simply being me." That's what I'm the most proud of in my life—that I haven't let others hold me back from living my happiest life. I've been true to myself and I am happy because of it.

Sunny Suggestions

1. Be fearless. One of my favorite songs is Taylor Swift's "Fearless." It's about letting go of the nerves and the potential risk of failure. Who cares? The happiest people are the ones who are willing to go out on a limb to reach for what they want in life. It's time you do the same! Sitting back in the shadows waiting for your life to happen has got to end. To make it happen you have to stop waiting and worrying. Be fearless and free.

Your Sunny Side: Are you living fearlessly when it comes to pursuing your passions or is something holding you back? What could that "something" be?

2.   Be proud! Sure, humble pie tastes delicious but every now and then you've got to have some proud pie, too. When you're aware of what you've accomplished in your life, you'll be that much more encouraged to keep going for the gold. Sometimes we all need a little positive reinforcement and having the proof that we've performed well in the past can be the added confidence and happiness booster we all need.

Your Sunny Side: What are five things you are proud of in your life?

1. _____

2. _____

3. _____

4. _____

5. _____

3.   Reward yourself. When you've earned something, party up your success by going to a nice dinner or spending time with your friends. Recognize your hard work and celebrate those that helped you along the way. There are enough challenges in life so we need to play up the positive. Whenever anything great happens in your life or someone special's life— make it a big deal. When you've done well, you'll be happy already but when you make a celebration out of it, you'll be twice as happy and you'll remember it all the more.

Your Sunny Side: How can you turn your successes into fun festivities?

_____

_____

Let Your Setbacks Be Your Start-Up

One reason it's so important to recognize success is because there will be times when success doesn't come so easily. We all have our challenges in one way or another and if you let them, they can be one of the greatest threats to happiness. But no matter what we've experienced in the past, we can't let our setbacks prevent us from pursuing our passions, and ultimately our happiness. When we let our hardships hold us back from our goals, we are stifling so much potential success and joy in life. It is not about the way we are challenged, but how we chose to overcome those challenges.

Sunny Samples

1. Mia: "Last summer, I was on the diving team. At the time, diving was the most exciting thing I'd ever done and I had so much fun each day. But when it came to high dive, I just couldn't get over my fear of heights. I would stand on the diving board staring at the water for a solid five minutes and end up climbing down the ladder. As I climbed down, I could clearly see my coach's disappointment. I don't think I've ever been so mad at myself before. I hated myself for not being able to dive off that 3-meter board. Days went by with me just standing up there, and my disappointment and frustration grew bigger each day. Then one day, my coach told me to just have fun and gave me the biggest hug of my life. It was like the entire wall I was building around me collapsed. It was nice to finally let go of my fear. And sure enough, I dived off that 3 meter."

2. Jessie: "There are a lot of challenges with my hobbies, but I think the hardest is when my family isn't proud of my photography, or they tell me that I'm not serious about my passions. I still don't have all the equipment or knowledge I need to truly call myself a photographer, and even though my family doesn't quite understand the importance of the equipment, I know that every time I create photos with what I have, they come out great. I have the raw talent. I just need to save my money now!"

3. Laurie: "I was challenged with acting earlier this year. I was the lead in one of the plays at the high school, and I struggled with the articulation of the lines. While it didn't come out to be as perfect as I had imagined, it was still extremely rewarding to get better at it and really challenge myself. I cannot say I was happy while doing it, but after the fact I was very happy that I had not given up."

4. Vince: "Not many people know this, but around my junior year in high school, I thought about giving up basketball. It was an awkward stage in my life, and I thought that it was a waste of my time because I didn't see a future in it. I wasn't improving fast enough to really enjoy the sport. It was a hard decision to make because I had been playing for three years and giving it up would mean throwing away three years of work. In the end I decided not to give up on myself and I worked hard to improve. It paid off and I am happy with my choice."

5. Erin: "It was really difficult for me not to make the cross country team at my university, but I kept pushing and earned a spot for the next year. That which does not kill us makes us stronger."

Our setbacks can leave us feeling lost at sea. We have to remember that we can grow stronger every day as we survive our personal storms. Whether you see it or not, the sun is always shining. It may not be shining on you all the time, but it is there, even behind the clouds. Life is constantly changing and as the seasons of your life come and go, the sun will always be there. We just have to believe it will shine in good time.

Sunny Suggestion

Don't let yourself forget. It can be easy to get caught up in our current challenges but there's nothing more encouraging than knowing we have a record of conquering our fears and overcoming our struggles. It's important to remind yourself of these memories—especially when life is getting you down and you feel like it's the end of your world. Put your dilemma in perspective by looking back on your past successes.

Your Sunny Side: Describe three instances when you had a challenge or setback but you were able to overcome it.

1. _____

2. _____

3. _____

And Don't It Feel Good?

Enough doom and gloom. Let's get back to the sunny side. Everyone has their own definition of fun but we all spell it the same way. If you ever need some inspiration when you're bored, here's a great list of "fun" activities for some instant happiness. You can always find something to do if you put a little mental elbow grease into it. Here's how many of you define fun—I doubt Webster's can pinpoint it like this.

Sunny Samples

1. Andy: "During my spare time, I LOVE going to the beach with friends. Whether we're relaxing on the sand or bodysurfing in the waves, I find it fulfilling. I also enjoy going on adventures to new places, traveling, shopping, reading, listening to music, swimming, spending time with family and friends, watching movies, and simply relaxing."
2. Michelle: "I hang out with friends. We always look for something new to try, like picking blueberries at a farm or going to an art gallery in downtown. But then again, it's more about the people I'm with than what we are actually doing. Even if we are cleaning up trash on the beach, if I am with people that I care about, then anything can be fun."
3. Sam: "People watching! I know it is random, but it takes your mind off yourself and lets you explore the world of others. And who knows, you might make a friend or two."

4. Jessie: "I like to do something in the moment, like going to Disneyland out of the blue. I have fun going on adventures, or getting lost while on adventures! Whether it's by myself or with friends, I usually have a great time sharing an adventure with someone."

5. Tiana: "I love going out and playing golf. I've played since I was very little and I've learned that even though it is always a challenge for me, it is also very relaxing. It clears my mind of everything and I focus on the moment."

6. Kurt: "Music, as a whole, makes me happy. When I play my guitar and randomly pluck away at strings, I have a sense of peace, and for a while I don't worry about anything else. Even listening to music that I enjoy can easily bring a smile to my face. I also like to write my own songs. When I finish writing a song it's a fantastic sense of accomplishment."

7. Emma: "I love to run for several reasons. One is to train, one is to explore, one is to see beautiful places, one is to challenge myself, one is to exercise, and one is because it's my alone time. It allows me to clear my head. I also love to talk with friends. I have an analytical personality and I enjoy trading opinions and learning new things. I love to read because I love to learn and I love getting lost in stories. I love to cook. I eat a lot of healthy food and I love the process of cooking my own meals, experimenting, and making it taste great."

8. Mia: "Swimming makes me happy. I think it's because when I'm swimming, I'm in my own world. I don't have to worry about homework or what happened at home. It gets my mind off things. When I'm swimming I just have to focus on getting to that wall. After a long day, it's nice to have that deep inner peace with the solitude that water brings."

9. Ben: "Traveling is one of my biggest passions. I am not the type of person to sit still. I like to go everywhere and explore. Unfortunately college expenses come before travel expenses, but traveling is worth it every time."

10. Leah: "Two hobbies make me extremely happy. The first is playing music. Whenever I feel confused or upset about anything, I sit down at the piano and play. I play Broadway show tunes, Disney songs, or contemporary songs, and they all make me feel so happy. I can't exactly explain why playing music makes me happy...there's something about it that is thrilling to me. The second hobby of mine is acting. I don't do this as often, but acting on stage allows me to express what another person might be thinking. I love becoming a different person and being able to experience something completely different than what I feel every day."

Sunny Suggestions

1.   The 70/30 Rule. I think 60% of our time should be spent toward our academics, our work and tasks at hand. The other 40% is for fun. When we're striving toward something meaningful, we're definitely earning some points on our happiness credit score. But what good would life be if we never bought anything special with our hard earned points? With as much work as you put in, eventually you have to reap the benefits. And that's where the 40% comes in--you have to have fun at some point. If you don't do something to enjoy the happiness you've earned, it starts to have an expiration date. Work hard to be happy, not just to make money.

Your Sunny Side: What do you think your current happiness balance is and why?

_____

_____

How can you implement balance between work and play?

_____

_____

2.   Write down 10 things that are fun—things that you *love* to do. It's the first step toward not only finding a career that you may enjoy some day, but what will make you happy, *today*. This is a great list to fall back on if you hit a road bump or you find yourself stagnating and unable to express your happiness. Make your list on first instincts—don't think about it too much.

Your Sunny Side: What exactly do you like to do for fun?

1. _____

2. _____

3. _____

4. _____

5. _____

6. _____

7. _____

8. _____

9. _____

10. _____

3.   Now think bigger. You've got your list of 10. But the more we grow, the happier we are. It's time to get creative with your life and work outside of the box. Stretch yourself—expand your possibilities. By writing down five new things you think *could* be fun, you'll be opening yourself up to new ideas that you may never have even thought about. Hopefully, at this point in the book, you'll be feeling a little braver when it comes to trying new things. This list you're about to write could be a great first step. With so much potential happiness out there, don't you think it's time to pursue some new activities?

Your Sunny Side: What are five things you've always wanted to do for fun but just haven't gotten around to yet? After you read this book, it's time to go out and do it!

1. _____

2. _____

3. _____

4. _____

5. _____

I encourage you to find some fun as much as possible—make it perfect every day in your own practical way. We can't all go to cooking school in France or go skiing in the Swiss Alps on a whim. But that doesn't mean we can't create our own adventures every day. We've got to modify our lives while we keep striving for our ultimate goals. You can have happiness right now—it doesn't have to be something to anticipate in the future. By incorporating a little more fun and a lot more passion in your life, you'll start seeing a notable difference in your happiness score.

Our quote this chapter is by Joseph Addison, an eighteenth century writer and politician:

"Three grand essentials to happiness in this life are something to do, something to love and something to hope for."

Are you living your life like this? Are you loving what you do, loving the people around you, and loving what you have to look forward to in the future. When your future goals go with your gut feeling, you'll feel so much more fulfilled in your studies, your work, and your relationships. Your happiness is a natural by-product when your passions and the people you love come into play.

Perhaps you're leaving this chapter feeling like you need to shake up your life a little more. This is your chance! Go out there and do what you love. There is no better time to try out new experiences. Find your like-minded friends, or heck, take a leap of faith and do something alone just because YOU love to do it—no matter how many are in your company—follow your hobbies to find your happiness.

Tim McGraw always says to "live like you're dying." Sure, thinking this way can spur us to action, but how about live like you're ALIVE? This is your time, your living and breathing moments you won't be able to get back. We never know when those final breaths will come. Use the breath that you have now to see the world, love with all your heart, and have the happiness that is right here waiting for you on this earth.

A Tale of Two Hearts

"It was the best of times, it was the worst of times; it was the age of wisdom, it was the age of foolishness; it was the epoch of belief, it was the epoch of incredulity; it was the season of Light, it was the season of Darkness; it was the spring of hope, it was the winter of despair; we had everything before us, we had nothing before us; we were all going directly to Heaven, we were all going the other way."

Even though this quote, in the introduction of Charles Dickens' *A Tale of Two Cities* describes France's Revolutionary War, I don't think there could be a better quote to describe young love. Our relationships can offer us the most indescribable moments of happiness but they can also leave us feeling emptier than grandma's cookie jar. There is nothing like a first love; because of it, your life is forever changed. You just have to be careful that it is changed in the right way.

I've thought a lot about this chapter. Maybe because love has left a lasting impression on my not-so-long life and I know it has for many of you as well. Whether you're single, in a long-term relationship, suffering from a broken heart, or playing the field like Beckham, I've had many people tell me that their intimate relationships have affected their happiness more than any other aspect of their life.

I can relate. I've been the crazy-in-love girl with the goo-goo eyes and swooning smile but I've also been the girl who cried harder than I ever thought possible after leaving a four-year relationship. I've been jaded before and I've been hopeful before. I've been lonely, even in love, and I've been single by choice and not by choice. And while I won't deny that I tend to be somewhat of a serial monogamist, I feel like I've walked in just about every pair of shoes—at least a few miles or so. I feel like it's important to share my history with you so that we can come from a place of mutual understanding. More than anything, I want to relate with you, not preach to you. I am just like the rest. The stories I share with you, along with the stories of numerous other young adults, are here to help all of us understand each other better. If we want to lead happier lives, it's time we start talking. So let's talk—about everything. I promise I won't be shy with you like one of those awkward parents with the fogged up glasses and tight waistbands. It's time to be real and say it like it really is. Does being in love make us happier people?

For some people, that's an obvious answer: of course you're happier when you're in love. But even if love adds to our happiness, we should still be able to experience just as much joy in our lives when we're single. It's not healthy to rely on another person to make you happy. It's all about your mindset. Sure, being single can be lonely if you make it that way. Especially when it feels like all of your friends have someone to call late at night and all you have is your teddy bear to talk with. But remember—other people can't always make you happy, you make your own happiness. This is a crucial point to understand and remember. No matter what your relationship status, your well-being comes from within. Here's what you had to say about the single life.

Sunny Samples

1. Elaine: "When I am single I'm happy because I have so much time for my girlfriends and I spend more time on improving myself; reflecting, studying, researching, going home to visit my family. But when I'm in a committed relationship, nothing beats that companionship. I can't decide which is better."

2. Carmen: "Well I have been in a four-year relationship and I have been very happy, but before I met my boyfriend I was just as happy. I have always

had great friends and an amazing family support system so I have never felt like I 'needed' to be in a relationship to be happy.

3.   Lindsay: "Currently, I do not feel happy as a singleton. I feel that I am missing out on something by never having had a boyfriend before. Sure I have been on something like a date and I had what I thought was a resemblance of a relationship, but it never turned into anything significant. Nor do I feel like the men I was involved with were truly interested in me. Alcohol played a role in one relationship and the other was meant to be a 'Friend with Benefits' relationship. Both went awry. During these instances I thought I was happy but when I realized the true nature of the relationships, my happiness was shattered. Following both I felt heartbroken, even though I was the one who let both go too far. As a single woman in general, I do not currently feel happy. I feel lonely and in a way, broken. Broken not because of a broken heart but because I feel as if something is wrong with me that keeps the boys away. I tell myself that this idea is ludicrous, but as the days, months, and years keep passing by, the idea roots itself a little deeper into my mind, to the point where I worry if I will ever have a boyfriend."

4.   Sara: "At this point in my life I'm happier being single because the only boyfriend I've had was a controlling ass. He would make fun of the things I wore and I always had to 'look my best.' I like being able to do what I want, go where I want, and hang out with whomever I want. I like being an independent woman."

5.   Dylan: "It's hard to give a simple answer because saying that one person makes me happy implies that other people don't. I have been single for a long time and I've had some of my happiest moments during that time. But I would say I am the happiest in a committed relationship, because it gives you a sense of security knowing that, no matter what happens to you outside of the relationship, you always have someone who you can talk to or just be with to forget about it all."

So based on these responses, are we happier in love? It depends on the person you are with, and how dependent you are on other people. But it's all about your *perspective*: rather than sulk about your status, take your bachelor/bachelorette standing as an opportunity for self-discovery. Learn about who you are. Establish goals for yourself, discover what your passions are, and take the time to pursue those interests. The great thing about being single is that you no longer have to worry about making sure your partner is happy; instead, you can discover what makes *you* happy. And who knows? When you're doing what you love, you just may run into someone who loves to do exactly the same thing, and just like that you've met your match.

Sunny Suggestions

1.   Get rich—in happiness. Of course there is great happiness to be had in bringing joy to the people that you love the most. But there is just as much happiness to be had when you give it to yourself. My mom has a great metaphor that she has shared with me over the years. It goes like this: There is a poor man on the street asking another man for a million dollars. The man says he wishes that he could give him the money but he can't give it to him because he doesn't have a million dollars in the first place. Well the same goes for love. We can't truly love someone if we do not have love within ourselves first. We can't make someone happy unless we are happy ourselves. There is nothing to give if we don't have something to offer in the first place.

Your Sunny Side: At this point in time, if you had to rate yourself in happiness and love for yourself between zero and one million dollars, how much would you give yourself and why?

_____

_____

How can you invest in yourself to increase your self-worth?

_____

_____

2. Push yourself outside of your comfort zone. I know it can be challenging to go beyond your boundaries but studies have repeatedly shown that we are happier when we challenge ourselves, even if it feels frightening, awkward or daunting at first. Even the philosopher Kant knew in the 1700's that it was the "higher quality pleasures" like pursuing an education, following a challenging career, and visiting someplace new that offered more happiness in life. Watching TV or zoning out on the Internet just ain't gonna cut it. So take the opportunity to turn off the TV, to log off Facebook, and to silence your cell phone. Discover what will make you the happiest, even when you're alone and when you're away from all the gizmos.

Your Sunny Side: What are five new things do to as a singleton that will add to your happiness?

1. _____

2. _____

3. _____

4. _____

5. _____

What are three benefits of your being single? (Answer this even if you're in a relationship!)

1. _____

2. _____

3. _____

3. Be with your friends! Many of us have felt guilty (myself included) for ignoring our friends when we're in a relationship. And guess what? Most of our friends can quickly become acquaintances if we don't invest the time they deserve. Let your friends know how much you care about them by spending quality time with them—whether you're single or not. Even though an exciting new relationship can make us extremely happy, so can our friends and they still deserve just as much credit.

Your Sunny Side: What are some fun things you can do with your friends that you can't do with your boyfriend or girlfriend?

To sum it all up: whether you're single or your friends are single, remember that a relationship status shouldn't define your happiness. People can add to our happiness, but they do not define it. Only we have that power. You have a responsibility to yourself to be happy, with or without a partner. Until you have this happiness, and a love for yourself, it'll be a much greater struggle to bring happiness or love to another, especially your special someone.

The Daily Miracle

When you are in love, it can seem that there is nothing more thrilling. When I asked people if they'd ever been in love before, if they had, their enthusiasm was nearly indescribable. Almost everyone would preface their comment with, "I know it sounds cliché" or "I know it seems cheesy, but..." But if you're a hopeless romantic like I am, then you'll know that love doesn't have to be cliché or sappy sweet—we can just enjoy it for what it is. In fact, I think love is something of a miracle in this day and age. How is it not miraculous to have such a special relationship with a person who was once a complete stranger? Don't you think it's just a little magical that one of the most important people in our lives was once someone who we may have just passed by on the street—without having the faintest idea that they would one day be our best friend and the love of our lives? I love that. You never know what a day will bring. Here's what some of you had to say about love.

Sunny Samples

1. Julia: "I am in love right now! I thought I knew what love was in high school, but I had it all wrong. There are no words that can truly describe how happy I am now. Just like the movie *Moulin Rouge* suggests: 'The greatest thing you'll ever learn is just to love and be loved in return.' I believe that with all my heart. I am ecstatic that I get to share everything in my life with one person. The person I love is always there for me, never gets angry with me, loves the person I am, and thinks I am the most beautiful person he has ever seen. I feel so many things: relief, excitement, fear, and bliss. Love has created the happiest state I have ever been in and I never want to let it go."

2. Peter: "I have been in love twice in my life, at least by my standards of love. The two relationships were very different, under very different circumstances, and yet the feeling seems to transcend both stories. It is hard to truly describe being in love, other than as a heightening of all emotions. The majority of the time, it heightened the feelings of happiness and joy in life. You appreciate things so much more because you share experiences with someone who, at the time, made your life complete."

3. Delaney: "Yes, I have been in love before and each time it's to a different degree. Each time a relationship ends, you have the chance to be that much more grateful for the next one. Love is a temporary euphoria. Nothing else matters and every moment is spent thinking of the person who holds your heart. It is such a gift and I am thankful that I've experienced it, regardless of the pain of losing that person or not."

4. Carmen: "I met my boyfriend as a freshman, but we were only friends at first. Now, it's been four years, and I am deeply and passionately in love with him. Our love grows every day, and I have been fortunate enough to fall in love with my best friend. We have no secrets and we are completely ourselves, flaws and all. I am happy every day with him. Even if there is something bad going on in one of our lives or we argue, I am still just as happy and in love as ever."

5. Steven: "I'm in love right now! I'm so madly in love that I moved from the Pacific Coast all the way to the Atlantic Coast to bring my relationship to the next level. The feeling of happiness that he gives me is indescribable and unlike anything I've ever felt before. Even though we have our arguments we love each other unconditionally."

I've been in this kind of love before. The kind that seems everlasting, unending, and abounding—and you remember it that way, even after it has ended. That is the beauty of true love. Even when it is gone, we take it with us wherever we go. There is no bitterness, no resentment—just gratitude for what once was. And we have no regrets, either. This is a good place to be and I'm thankful that I am now in that place.

Love changes each time we have a new relationship. Each person you love shows you a new kind of happiness, a new kind of perspective on life that only they could show you in such an intimate way. In my first relationship, I experienced fearless love, the kind in which you are entirely trusting—and completely enamored. It was perfect—I even thought we would get married. But I was 16 years old at the time and 16 became 18; and with this passage of time, the passion passed on as well. While this naturally happens to a degree with all relationships, we just grew apart too much. At such a young age you both are changing and we realized: it was time to let it go.

I've since moved on to my second relationship, where I've taken a much more practical approach. Being crazy in love makes you want to be sane in love, so this time I am. I didn't want to be in a relationship that was all consuming; I wanted to live my own life this time. It feels much healthier and yet I am just as happy. Time will tell where our relationship takes us but no matter what the outcome, I will always be grateful for the lessons I've learned from both of my relationships. No matter what your experience with love has been like, here are some Sunny Suggestions to make your love the happiest it can be.

Sunny Suggestions

1. **Don't hold back.** Don't let your love get lost—whether you meet someone who interests you or you're already with someone you love, make sure the person knows how you feel. It's better to say everything you want them to know, even if you risk embarrassment or rejection. You then don't live with a "what if" cloud hanging over your head for who knows how long. I don't believe in coincidences—we're presented with certain people for a reason. Don't let them pass you by.

Your Sunny Side: What can you do to cherish your love more?

_____

_____

2. **Know the Rubber Band Theory.** We all need our space—otherwise we'll start to suffocate. Like a rubber band, sometimes we all need to pull back a little bit to maintain our independence. But when we take our space, we're stronger when we come back together—just like that forceful pull of a rubber band once it's been pulled in two directions. I learned about this in John Gray's book, *Men Are From Mars, Women Are From Venus*. The concept might sound odd at first, but think about it—no one wants to be the cling-on waiting by the phone, begging for attention. Be your own person and *then* be together. Don't lose yourself in your relationship.

Your Sunny Side: Do you maintain your individuality in your relationship? If not, how can you work on establishing and continuing your independence?

_____

_____

3. Speak Love Languages. I'm a huge fan of Dr. Gary Chapman's book, *The Five Love Languages*. No matter what language you speak, we can all understand and give love languages. Whether it's with words of affirmation, quality time, gifts, acts of service, or physical touch, it's important that we make sure the people we love *feel* loved. You can love someone but you won't necessarily make them happier unless you express it in a way that they can relate. I highly encourage you to go to Dr. Chapman's website and take the online test. To become fluent in the five types of "love languages" he identifies, here's a little preview:

- **Words of Affirmation**: This person appreciates kind comments both in person and in the written word. They'll love a nice card or Facebook comment and they especially like hearing an "I love you," when it's sincere of course! These people tend to be genuine, sincere, and heart-felt. They wear their heart on their sleeve and they're not afraid to be emotional.

- **Quality Time**: This person is a "yes man," a doer, a go-getter. They like adventure and they want their loved ones to be along for the ride. They don't like to spend much time alone and they prefer to bond over shared activities. These people can be outgoing, sharing, and thoughtful. They like to invite others along but don't forget to include them as well!

- **Gifts**: This person is creative, appreciative, and tries to enjoy all that life offers. They love a well-thought-out gift because it means you understand them. Gifts are not necessarily financial tokens; rather they are symbols of affection and love to this person. They like the little things in life. It's not about the gift itself, but rather the thought that went into giving it.

- **Acts of Service:** The busy person loves this kind of appreciation. In fact, it's often parents who find this type of love to be the most rewarding. But even if you don't have children, you may still relate because at their core, this person values compassion, perceptiveness, and initiative. People who enjoy acts of service love when others have a keen sense of awareness. It's doing the dishes when they have a test to study for or making them dinner when they're sick. When someone is overwhelmed or stressed they may have trouble communicating how they need help but when you are receptive to their needs without always being given specific instructions, it will be greatly appreciated.

- **Physical Touch:** This person is the ageless romantic—they always have a spark about them. They are honest, genuine, and enjoy the comfort of others. For them this form of affection shouldn't be forced; it should come naturally and when it does, it is greatly accepted. Whether it's a quick kiss or something more passionate, they love making a connection.

Can you especially relate with any of these languages? Furthermore, if you have someone in your life, do you have a sense of what love language they may speak? For a more in depth guide, I recommend reading Dr. Chapman's book yourself, but this is a great start. Once you begin thinking about how you can give love rather than just get it all the time, your happiness is sure to follow. There is nothing more endearing or pleasing than to see how you have made your partner happy.

Your Sunny Side: Which of the Five Love Languages do you think you speak?

_____

_____

How do you think you can express love with each of the following languages?

1. Words of Affirmation:

_____

_____

The Sunny Side Up!

2. Quality Time:

_____

_____

3. Gifts:

_____

_____

4. Acts of Service:

_____

_____

5. Physical Touch:

_____

_____

God Bless The Broken Road

Now I hate to be the one to break the bad news, but the truth is, most relationships at this age will probably end in a breakup. Don't get me wrong, I'm happy if you're happy with your high school heartthrob but usually the football deflates and the crown from homecoming night tarnishes. But I hope the potential for love lost won't hold you back from love to be had. Alfred Lord Tennyson said, "It is better to have loved and lost then to never have loved at all." So much of the time, true happiness comes when we've risked our safety blanket for the possibility of something splendid.

Even if it may not last forever, you shouldn't go through your life without ever experiencing love.

I'll admit, breaking up with anyone, whether it was a boyfriend or a best friend, has brought some of the unhappiest periods in my life. I never like saying goodbye to anyone, even when I know that the relationship is no longer beneficial to either person. I remember feeling so old and tired after my first break-up. I was only 18 and I already felt so jaded. Thinking to myself of Taylor Swift's lyrics, "Why do we bother with love if it never lasts?" It's a fair question. I remember being so madly in love and then watching it slowly die. Feeling the gnaw of doubt that eventually left a hole in me. We all change, especially in these years of our lives, but then must love change as well?

After seeing so many parents divorce, after watching our friends get betrayed, how do we find the faith to love freely and without holding back? I think there's one simple answer: the pursuit of happiness. It's what every person wants when they make themselves vulnerable to love. Love can offer us our greatest moments of joy. Even with the potential risks that come with a relationship, we are willing to put it all on the line for the potential happiness that love can bring.

When that love ends, as it sometimes does, it can be devastating. Just the sheer comfort and security of knowing that your partner will always be there for you is suddenly *gone*. It's jarring. It's shocking. It's unsettling. Whether you were broken up with or you broke up with someone often makes little difference; the pain is still there. Because let's face it…as much as we may say it, it's rare to "still be friends."

Even though lasting relationships at this age are hard to come by, it's still important to remember how much we can learn from our relationships. There is always something positive to take away from a broken relationship, even if the only positive thing is the strength to walk away.

Sunny Samples

1. Michaela: "I have never felt happy when I broke up with a boyfriend, but I knew that it was not what I was looking for so I ended an inevitable ending early, with less room for deep feelings to evolve. When I was broken up with, however, I was devastated. I thought that everything was fine, and he made no hints that things were anything but perfect. It was unexpected and on top of that, it was a very juvenile break up on his part. That hurt me, but it made me realize that what we had was not special. And I ultimately found my current boyfriend because of it. So things happen for a reason, there is a soul mate out there for all of us I truly believe."

2. Brian: "I have broken up with someone before, but my story is a little different. I was in a committed relationship with a girl for almost two years, but I broke up with her because I wasn't being honest with myself about my personal preference. When we broke up and I was able to start seeing boys I felt like a weight had been lifted, but at the same time, I felt terrible knowing that I hurt this girl in such a severe way."

3. Danielle: "I have experienced both sides of the spectrum of breakups. To be honest, whether I find myself being broken up with or breaking up with someone, it is always sad. This is not to say that it necessarily takes away my happiness, because I understand that this choice is what is best for that period of my life. If I know the relationship isn't working and I end things, I am sad for the loss but I am happy to know that I have the strength to move on. If I am broken up with, I am sad because my heart is still in a huge part of the relationship. Yet I know I would never want to be with someone who didn't want to be with me. So, in the end I am content with breaking up because I know there is someone who will appreciate what I have to offer and be grateful for it."

Breaking up is never easy. There is almost always someone that gets hurt, if not both parties. But you have to ask yourself, am I truly happy in this relationship? I believe that we are responsible for our own happiness. But in our intimate relationships, our partners should mainly be adding to that happiness rather than detracting from it. Of course, there will be arguments, and times of trial, but you have to weigh the overall pros and cons. When a relationship is no longer healthy or happy, what you ultimately want to do is your choice. But keep in mind: this is the beauty of our age. We are not usually feeling trapped by a marriage, children, or a mortgage payment. Usually, if we want them to be, our strings are pretty detachable. The cut is never easy, but nonetheless it can still be cut. Like a starfish, we can regrow after we lose a part of ourselves. So when should you break up? And when should you stick it out?

Sunny Suggestions

1. You find yourself rationalizing the relationship. Do you think with your head instead of your heart? This kind of thinking can lead to practical, idealized happiness rather than a genuine happiness, especially when it comes to love. For example, are you with this person because you think they will offer a promising future—when really, you're not happy in the present moment? Happiness is here, in the now—not just the next twenty years. If you're thinking more about who you want your partner to be, instead of who they are right now, there might be a problem. Or let me be blunt, there is a problem.

Your Sunny Side: Do you live in the present moment with your partner or are you constantly living in the hope of a better future?

_____

_____

2. You have a gut feeling. It's just there and it won't go away. Like a nagging fly that keeps swirling around your face, you can't deny your gut feelings no matter how hard you try. Just get the fly swatter and call it quits. In fact, much of the time the pitting feeling of your intuition, telling you what to do, takes away from your happiness more than the actual break-up. Trust me, I've been there. Don't waste these precious years of your life teetering on the fence. Pick which side you want to be on.

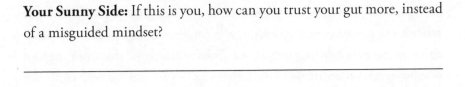

Your Sunny Side: If this is you, how can you trust your gut more, instead of a misguided mindset?

_____

_____

3. **Your friends and your family don't approve.** I know it can seem romantic to have a star-crossed love affair equivalent to R and J. But honestly, your family and friends may know you better than you know yourself—especially the parts of yourself that you might like to deny or ignore. Don't be afraid to ask your family and friends what they honestly think about your relationship. And be ready to hear the truth, even if it's not what you want to hear. Chances are they care about your well-being and your happiness, even if that means disapproving of your newest romance. Even if you disagree, you may still want to give their side a say.

This means that the people who are closest to you have a tremendous responsibility. If they really care about your happiness, then they should be willing to give you the tough love you might need. Let them be assured they can be honest with you. Be certain they know you are open to hearing their thoughts. And ideally, you should ask for your family and friends' advice before you get too seriously involved.

Still, at the end of the day, it is your decision and it is your happiness that you have to consider. If you are truly happy and you know in your heart that a certain person in your life is the right person for you at this time, then that is your choice. Use your head to listen to reason, but use your heart to feel what is right.

Your Sunny Side: Do you think your family and friends would offer you sound advice on your relationships? How much does their opinion matter to you?

_____

_____

4. Like an old pair of Converse shoes, it's just worn out. Most relationships at this age just don't have a long-lasting fabric. It's a sad truth to admit, but nonetheless, it is a truth. Some things just aren't built to last. You have to keep trying on pairs of shoes until you find the perfect fit. But that doesn't mean you shouldn't keep trying.

5. Leave immediately if the relationship is abusive. As I've witnessed with friends, ending an abusive relationship seems obvious, but this is easier said than done. But in case there are any questions, it is NEVER okay, negotiable, or within reason for your partner to harm you emotionally, verbally, sexually, or physically. Whether you are enduring 'Common Couple Violence'—where either partner hits, slaps, kicks, etc., or you are suffering from Intimate Terrorism, where your partner has cool and calculated control over you by threatening, aggressive, even life-threatening action—you should remove yourself at once, or as soon as you can. Here are some samples from people who've been there.

(Not So) Sunny Samples

1. Arielle: "I have been in two abusive relationships, one verbally and one sexually abusive, and this destroyed my happiness for the duration of our time together, and for a long time after. In both situations, my self-esteem and confidence took a nosedive. I must say that it was harder to be in a verbally/emotionally abusive relationship because the abuse was so much more obvious. Being sexually abused can be more easily hidden and thus is harder to identify (with the exception of violence, of course). But when someone makes it their goal to make you feel bad about yourself, and you let them, it is very hard to learn to be happy again."

2. Chloe: "I have been in a very unhealthy relationship that I created and invested in. Unrequited love is something a lot of people deal with, and it's hard to move on. I spent many years of my life 'loving' a friend of mine, trying to make something out of nothing. This stress and depression I brought on myself made me an unfocussed and unhappy person throughout middle school and high school. I was constantly getting jealous or upset because I didn't get what I wanted, even though I knew it would never happen. I'm still not sure why it was so hard for me to move on. The only thing that helped me, was not seeing the person every day. I know I created a mess for myself, but it was a good learning experience and I became a stronger and wiser person in the end."

3. Mary: "We all have experienced some kind of unhealthy relationship; I feel we may subject ourselves to this as part of the learning process we all partake in. We need to see the hurtful side of a relationship to understand and appreciate the true love in a relationship."

As hard as it can be to find the strength to walk away from whatever harmful situation you may be in, trust that your family and friends will get you through any difficult time. You are never alone and you can always ask for help. In fact, you *should* ask for help. Don't ever suffer in silence. You need to let yourself be happy—even if it means being without the person who means so much to you. It is your right.

Please call the National Domestic Hotline Association if you ever need help or advice: **1-800-799-SAFE (7233)**.

Playing at the Hookey Rink

I took a really interesting class my sophomore year in college called "Intimate Relationships" with Dr. Benjamin Karney. It's probably one of the most valuable classes I've taken and I've applied so many of the concepts I learned to my own relationships. One thing I found to be especially interesting in the class was the "art" of hooking up. It's pretty well known that young adults are a little more hung up on hooking up than older generations were and I've always been interested by this—do we do it because we think it will make us happier? My gut feeling is a resounding NO.

Even though hooking up may be on the rise, it is clearly evident from research and surveys that many young adults prefer to be in a committed relationship if they find the right person. And when they do, these relationships can be just as serious, special, and committed as any adult relationship—there's something to be said for young love even though it doesn't always receive due credit. All the same, I wanted to give some due attention to hooking up because young adults are doing it enough that you have to wonder how it affects our happiness. I mean, there must be something there, right? In fact, according to Bogle's research in 2008, most college students date *after* they have hooked up with the person.

But as you may know from personal experience, many hook-ups don't lead to a second date, or even a first one. It could be because quick-handed hanky panky and booze tend to go hand in hand. And shocker—this is the biggest reason why young adults regret their decision to hook up. But what I find to be most interesting is that, according to Lambert, Kahn, and Apple in 2003, both men and women think that other people, besides themselves are having a better time hooking up than they are. Apparently, the grass is greener on the other side of the door. So if you are thinking that hooking up is making other people happy, you might want to think again. It's usually not as simple and carefree as it looks. Remember the movie Easy A? It's often a big fat farce so don't get duped into doing something you don't want to do.

Sunny Samples

1.   Steven: "I honestly don't think there is ever a way hooking up can bring true happiness. Physical relationships may bring pleasure, but unless commitment and trust are added, it's empty. If you are going to kiss a complete stranger, you might as well kiss a wall. True happiness comes from giving of oneself, without expectation of anything in return. Hooking up is simply a flesh and blood replacement for the physical side of love. It can be harmless, but I also think it is pointless. Anything worth having is worth waiting for, so why not wait for the one person who will want to make you, and not just themselves, happy?"

2.   Amanda: "Hooking up is something I am strongly against. I hooked up with one guy that was not my boyfriend and I immediately regretted it. It made me feel used and gross about myself. Fortunately I learned a lot from it and now I am able to respect my decisions a lot more. I don't believe that it brings happiness at all. For certain people, it probably brings temporary happiness but not in the end."

3. Andrea: "For me it makes the hole in my heart even bigger and makes the empty feeling worse because you know that no matter what happens you're nothing more to the other person than a hookup."

Perhaps some gain happiness from their hookups but it just seems that there is so much more happiness to be had from a genuine relationship. The biggest reason? Trust. When you hook up with someone, you are sacrificing so much of yourself—not only your body but often your reputation. You don't want to be the Scarlet Letter of the library—even word gets around in college thanks to Facebook. And while not all rendezvous can lead to hurt feelings and broken promises, many of them do. One night's worth of "you're so beautiful" and "you're so hot" can quickly turn in to "he was terrible" or "she's a slut"—for everyone to hear and then blindly believe. Don't get me started on sexually transmitted diseases or unexpected pregnancy. Not that a relationship can necessarily save you from any of that, but when you're in a committed relationship, you can better assess whether or not your partner can be trusted.

Sunny Suggestion

Have a stance. Know how you feel about hooking up, otherwise it might happen to you unintentionally. If you know your limits, it's much less likely that you'll end up in a situation where you feel uncomfortable. If you have a standard policy that you can apply, lines won't get crossed and people will be more respectful to you (and probably more interested in you in the long run). Be sure of yourself and be confident in what you believe.

Your Sunny Side: So, all this said, how do you feel about hooking up?

_____

_____

How do you think hooking up will affect your happiness?

_____

_____

If you have hooked up in the past, how did you feel afterward?

_____

_____

Your *Notebook* Moment

I promised you I'd be honest in this book, especially in this chapter. Relationships are a BIG deal, especially at this time in our lives. For this segment of the book, I've tossed and turned over how I want to present SEX (or if I even want to address it). I've got so many opinions tossing and turning in my head. Do I take the Puritan, Sarah Palin approach and act like the best protection is abstinence (clearly that method pays off...) or do I tell it like it is and recognize that over half of teens have had sex by the time they graduate from high school? Well, because I told you I'd be real with you Sunny Girl style, here's my side on the topic on S-E-X... in a nutshell.

The basics: Be safe. Be smart. And to protect your heart: don't do it unless you're in love. If you think sex will lead to love or happiness you just might want to wait. In fact, you should wait. Don't have sex as a favor, out of guilt, out of pressure, or out of revenge. If you're going to run to home base, do it because you genuinely love and care for that person. That is when true happiness is likely to come into both of your lives. When sex is only a component of a strong relationship, rather than the entirety of it, you will experience a stronger and more lasting bond. Much longer than a one night stand. If you're doing it just because you're curious, bored, or carefree, any temporary happiness you may feel probably won't last.

Most likely, once the night has passed, you'll be feeling guilt, regret, and worry.

I know you've heard it a million times but save sex for someone who is special to you. It's worth the wait. Of course sex can add happiness to your life, but only when it means something more than what's done on the mattress.

There's my fair share. Here's what you had to say about it.

Sunny Samples

1. Steven: "While the physical side of a relationship is important (you can't be in love with someone without being physically attracted to them), I feel like the emotional and mental sides of a relationship hold a much higher significance—that is where true happiness comes from. Relationships based solely on physical aspects cannot be defined as true love."

2. Jacie: "I feel like physical relationships are important. It offers a sense of vulnerability in a relationship in which you already has a strong emotional connection with your partner. However, without that emotional foundation, a physical relationship can't really bring that same sense of meaning."

3. Casey: "I think that emotional relationships come first, then physical. Fall in love with someone's soul and mind, then you can fall for their looks and body."

4. Rachel: "A physical relationship is very important to me; I like to be cuddled and held. Your physical interaction speaks volumes about the expectations and values of you and whom you are with. It can definitely make you happier, but it can also tear you apart. Your head, heart, and body all need to be aligned beforehand."

5. William: "Holding hands, hugging, kissing, sex, are really only methods by which two people affirm and reinforce a relationship, no matter how healthy it may be. To me, this affirmation is very important in a relationship, but only if there is something legitimate that is being reinforced. It's the special way of indicating to each other that your relationship is special."

Thus far in my life, I've been in two major relationships. Like I said, I'm a long time dater. If there's anything I've learned from my relationships, it's that you have to make time for them. You can't let the kisses just come and go. Greet each other warmly. Don't let each other leave without a heartfelt goodbye. Don't let anything be lost in translation. Here are some Sunny Suggestions to make your physical and emotional bond the happiest it can be.

Sunny Suggestions

1. Surprise them! Give your partner a hug when they're working hard, or reach for their hand so that they don't have to reach for yours every time. Get them tickets to see their favorite basketball team. Don't procrastinate expressing your affection. It's hard to be in love with a lazy person! It's easier to be in love with a mindful person who will make you feel like you matter.

Your Sunny Side: What are five ways you can surprise your partner?

1. _____

2. _____

3. _____

4. _____

5. _____

2. Say how you feel—a lot. This doesn't have to only be with your boyfriend or girlfriend. Tell people that you love them and care about them on a regular basis. Let them know how lucky and blessed you are to have them in your life, and tell them why they make a difference. Tell them how much happiness they bring you.

Your Sunny Side: How do you feel about expressing your feelings to others? Is this difficult for you to do? If so, how can you improve on letting others know that they are loved?

_____

_____

3.   **Initiate. Invite. Instigate.** Make sure that you offer fun outings and suggestions for your special someone. If they feel like they are constantly making all the plans, they'll burn out. Pull your weight by making plans some of the time. And when you are asked where you'd like to go out to dinner or what you'd like to do on a Sunday afternoon, "I don't know" or "I don't care" responses are not allowed. It's attractive when you have an opinion and when you can make up your mind. Care enough to care what's going on in your relationship.

Your Sunny Side: Does it feel as though you always make the plans or do you leave it to your partner? Is the choosing in balance?

_____

_____

What are three fun date ideas you can think of that are your OWN ideas?

1.   _____

2.   _____

3.   _____

What's Waiting For You

When you are ready for love, and you have found love, it is an indescribable feeling. It is what we've been waiting for. It's what they read about to us during circle time as kindergarteners and what we've seen in every Meg Ryan movie. It's the kind of love that you can't help but smile about, think about, and talk about every second of every day.

But let's have a reality check now. As great as this love is (for the whopping six months), long term relationships would never last if infatuation was the key element. There has to be an element of commitment and a fundamental friendship that can withstand even the worst arguments (because yes, even the best relationships go through conflict—and it's not a bad thing). One book that I absolutely love is Dr. Gottman's *7 Principles of Successful Marriages*. In his book, he stresses how important this friendship base is. When you have more than the 'hots' to build up your happiness, your relationship can give you a profound happiness that is not situational but rather, sustaining.

Here are some Sunny Samples of what so many of us are hoping for someday.

Sunny Samples

1.   Dylan: "I'm in my ideal relationship; I am in a committed relationship with a beautiful, smart, talented girl who makes me feel appreciated every day."
2.   Jill: "I want a relationship where I can feel comfortable enough to wear a hoodie and a ponytail and know he still thinks I'm beautiful. I want to be with someone where I don't have to put on an act. I would be the happiest because I would be completely myself."
3.   Isaac: "My ideal relationship is with a smart and confident girl who isn't afraid to show exactly who she is to me and to the world. I won't hide that she would have to at least slightly be like-minded when it comes to politics and religion, or at least be able to see both sides of an issue. She has to be able to laugh at herself, and admit when she's wrong. And she

must, MUST, not only feel that she can make a difference in the world, but wants to as well. My ideal relationship is a kind of omnipresent happiness, the type that doesn't need to be poked and prodded like a dying fire. It's a perpetual happiness that can be found just from seeing each other."

4.   James: "In an ideal relationship, there is no pressure. It's not changing who you are to fit another person of how you should be. Instead, it's two people who can coexist in ways that they couldn't exist apart. It's the ultimate feeling of happiness because it inspires a confidence in you that's indescribable. It's a balance between what you need and what you want, in every aspect of life."

5.   Polly: "In my ideal relationship, my partner would love everything about me, and I about him. He would be everything I'm not, in a complimentary, not conflicting, way. I would be extremely happy in this relationship because I would feel that I was making my partner happier than anyone else could make him."

Sunny Suggestion

Know your love. I've never been one of those people that have a checklist of what they will and will not accept in a partner, but it is good to know what will, one day, make you happy. Don't settle or sell yourself short—you can have the love you are looking for because you deserve happiness and someone out there deserves to be happy too, all thanks to you.

Your Sunny Side: What embodies a true love relationship to you?

_____

_____

Franklin P. Jones said: **"Love doesn't make the world go round. Love is what makes the ride worthwhile."**

I hope that one day you'll be able to experience the kind of love you never want to leave. A love that is _fearless_—even if you've been hurt before. A love in which you can trust the person, and have faith that the relationship will last. A love where you wake up with a smile on your face and you go to bed with an even bigger one. A love where you are kissed often, hugged frequently, and given the affection you want and deserve. A love with the *right* kind of surprises. A love that goes beyond physicality and instead focuses on the fundamental nature of your bond. A love that is centered on daily happiness rooted in commitment and desire. That is the kind of love that I hope you have in your life—*and live happily ever after.*

Friends: The Sunshine of Life

One of my daily mantras is that our friends are the sunshine of life. They keep us happy, they keep us strong, and they keep us experiencing life to the fullest. Our friends can be like an endless summer day of laughter and carefree fun. Time without them is like dark winter day—life seems so much duller when you're not cheering each other on or up. Friendship is truly one of life's greatest blessings. Best of all, a friend just *gets* us in ways that no one else can.

After a long day, it is our friends who can still make us laugh. They are the ones to bring us chicken noodle soup when we're sick and who'll remember our birthdays (and by that I mean more than a one sentence Facebook "Happy Birthday" comment). Yes, our friends should be the ones to tell us the truth, even when the truth hurts. They talk with us until it's much too late at night, they listen to us (again, until it's much too late at night), and they are happy when we are happy. Friendships are truly miraculous if you think about it—the idea that you could unexpectedly meet a perfect stranger who can become a perfect companion is something quite amazing. We can't ever take it for granted.

So here's a toast: may we always appreciate our friendships. May we continually express our gratitude for friendships. And may we always *make the time* for our friendships. People can come and go so quickly throughout life. If you don't try to hold on to them, you'll lose them faster than misplaced car keys. Friendships take an effort, especially when you're not interacting on a daily basis. They require humility, devotion and selflessness at a moment's notice. But if we make an honest effort, our friendships make us better and happier people.

I know my friends have made a tremendous impact on my life. I have one best friend in particular who has been by my side long before I even have memories of our friendship. Our parents took us to swimming lessons when we were babies; I was one, she was about six months. The rest is history. Our families came together through many common bonds: we were only children, our dads were pilots, and oh yeah, we had the same name. (That's always been my favorite part). For my whole life "Lauren & Lauren" have been a team and we have seen each other through backyard tree houses, middle school awkwardness, and high school sweethearts—birthday parties, graduations, and debutante balls. We've danced, baked cookies, and laughed the whole way through. We've traveled the country together with our families, packing into Lauren's dad's Cessna everywhere we went. Whether it was landing on the airport strip of Hearst Castle or flying to the beaches of Mexico—we jumped on every bed, went through a million pairs of walking shoes (or so it seemed), and we've been in just about every pool in California known to man. Through it all, we have been and always will be best friends.

I go into such great detail with this friendship because the memories matter. It is so important to recognize how they have added meaning and depth to your life along with how they impact you in the present. Lauren has been the sister I've never had and a better friend than I could have imagined and she will forever hold those places in my life. I always try to appreciate and foster this friendship, because it is truly a gift that keeps on growing. It's important to remember that friendships like these should always be nurtured, never neglected. Here's what you love about your friendships so much.

Sunny Samples

1. Lily: "My friends are my support system. I can depend on them, and they help me feel safe and cared for. They accept me for who I am and they

don't judge. I know they will always be there when I need them or I am feeling lonely. They also help me reduce stress. Not only do they listen to me when I need to vent, they also provide a much-needed diversion from what is stressing me out in the first place. Having a group of friends where I belong makes me a happier person."

2. Sarah: "They are the handful of people that are by your side when you're lonely, put a smile on your face when you're down in the slumps, hold your hand when you're heartbroken, and comfort you with hugs when you've lost hope. They are there for you, through thick and thin. You don't have to put up a façade or an Iron Man suit when you're with them."

3. David: "My friendships are the most important things in my life right now. My friends have always been there for me and no matter what happens, they help me through a lot of difficult times. I just enjoy being with my friends no matter what we're doing."

In honor of honoring your friends, here are some ways you can make your appreciation known. You don't have to get mushier than a microwaved peep (I don't recommend trying this by the way), but you should make your friends feel celebrated. If your friends make you so happy, don't you think you should do the same?

Sunny Suggestions

1. Surprise them with simple yet special gifts. It doesn't have to be extravagant. The most important thing is that it is personalized. When a friend knows that you have put time and effort, rather than just money, into selecting a gift, it will mean the world to them. I have a little policy for myself when it comes to getting gifts for my friends. Anytime I go out shopping, whether it's to the grocery store or mall, I always buy something for someone else. It can be something as simple as a box of Goldfish crackers for my roommate, or a catchy bracelet I thought a friend would like. Then I'll put the gift under their pillow or behind their backpack with a nice little note attached. I don't know if it's more fun waiting for them to see the surprise or watching them light up with a smile on their face when they discover it. I highly recommend you try it—it's one of the most special ways to show that you treasure a friend.

Your Sunny Side: What are a few ideas you have for surprising your friend and making them feel special?

_____

_____

_____

2.   **Write them a kind letter or leave them a message.** Don't you love when that notification button of Facebook pops up with a comment from a friend you haven't heard from in a while? Or better yet, when you get a letter in the mail that isn't from the bank or the phone company? Whether you mail them a letter or you just send a quick text message, words of love are always valued. Girls especially find this meaningful—I know that I often save every sweet letter, card, even post-it note that I'm given. Having something in the written word is a gift that lasts forever.

Your Sunny Side: Who are three friends that you would like to reach out to that could use a little extra TLC these days?

1.   _____

2.   _____

3.   _____

3.   **Plan an exciting event to do together.** Got a Disney fanatic for a friend? Put on the Mouse Ears and go! Have a pal who loves to paint? Let her teach you and go to an art class together. Sometimes the hardest part about a friendship is just coordinating the date, time, and place. So when

you go the extra mile to invite a friend to an activity that you've planned, even if it's just getting coffee or lunch, it will immediately express to your friend that they are not only worth your time and effort, but that you are will willing and wanting to be with them. The key here is to just have a solid plan. There's nothing worse than calling your friend and the two of you playing phone tag, "What do you want to do?" "I don't know; what do you want to do?" "I don't know; what do you want to do?" Don't be that friend. Know what you want to do—and invite your friend to join along.

Your Sunny Side: What are five fun "friend dates" you can think of?

1. _____

2. _____

3. _____

4. _____

5. _____

4. Give them a hug! Not all people are comfortable with physical affection, but for those who are, physicality can be a great way to bond. Even if it's something as simple as a high five or as complex as a secret handshake, physical touch can be especially meaningful when shared between friends. My teacher would sing in kindergarten, "four hugs a day; that's the minimum, not the maximum!" I think that's a good standard to have. You don't have to save hugs for special occasions—hug just to hug!

5. Do them a favor—without being asked. Is your friend too busy to take her dog for a walk? Take Pluto out around the neighborhood. Got a bud that's starved with no time to snag some grub? Go pick up some lunch for them. Showing that you are selfless and that your needs do not come first is a meaningful way to express how much you value your friendship.

A common complaint I hear from young adults is that they have many fair-weather friends who are great for a laugh, but run away the second a storm cloud rolls in. When your friend is going through a storm, or even when they're having a sunny day, offer to help them without expecting the favor to be returned. Let them know you have the time to help and that you want to support them.

Your Sunny Side: What are a few ways that you can help out a friend when they're stressed?

_____

_____

_____

I remember singing in the choir, "We're Blessed to Bless Again." It's the same for happiness: we are happy when we make others happy. It's a simple truth but if we make a daily effort to live by this notion, we will see the general demeanor of everyone improve. Be a blessing to others; be a ray of sunshine to your friends. Everyone wants that golden glow that comes from a fruitful friendship.

Time to Say Goodbye

But what about when your friends leave more of a sunburn on you than that nice healthy glow? It's sad to admit, but many of the friends we make in life are only temporary. Some just seem to slip away. With others, we have to deliberately choose to remove ourselves. When a friendship is no longer adding to either party's happiness, it may be time to let it go. Especially at this age, friendships can come and go faster than we'd like. People are discovering who they are and who they want to become. You and your friends may not always fit into each other's life plans. That's not to say that you can't keep in touch when the miles separate, but if your mindsets are dividing you, then it may be time to say goodbye. While it can be hard to accept, it is simply a sign that you have better, and truer, friends awaiting you. Don't let a bad-fit friend hold back your happiness any longer.

Our true friends are the ones we want to have by our sides throughout our life. Not just at the wedding, but also at the baby showers, the holiday parties and even when we're 80 at the bridge games. They are the friends who, no matter where they live, we will keep in touch with—those for which we will *always* make an effort. And while it is nice to have many friendly acquaintances with the people that surround you, it is crucial that we have our closest friends involved in our lives, through the sun and the rain, across the miles and through the years.

Still, it's never easy to lose a friend, even if they've only been your friend for two months. When I lost my closest friend in high school it was an extremely challenging time. I had never before felt so alone, which, as a self-conscious high school sophomore, was especially bad timing. The hardest part about it was feeling like I was the only one, in the entire school, without a best friend or even a close group of friends. Looking back, I realize this was a ridiculous idea—but at the time, it was very real for me.

I hope my story can serve as a reminder that we are never alone in our tough times. Even though it's not always verbalized or written with a sharpie on someone's forehead, everyone has a personal and private story that is their own. Everyone has a battle they're enduring; it's just that we're not usually soldiers on their field. We're fighting our own battles. But if we only knew, as I hope this book will show, we are never alone and there is always someone on our side of the trenches. With that sense of solace, we can start to find happiness from our hardships.

No one likes to be in conflict, especially with friends, but it does happen sometimes. No matter what the difference of opinion may be, it's important to ask yourself how much you value the friendship. And while I never recommend burning bridges with people, sometimes it is wiser to get off the bridge before falling into a moat of alligators that will eat you alive. I want to address this issue because having challenges with a friend can be one of the greatest happiness stealers, and I don't ever want you to feel robbed in your relationships. Sometimes you need to kindly excuse yourself from a friendship rather than be stuck feeling miserable. So when should you stay and when should you go?

Sunny Suggestions

1. **Ask yourself, "Can I see myself still being friends with this person beyond this experience that we are currently sharing together?"** If the answer is yes, then write a poem, sing a song, do a dance—do whatever it takes to keep your friendship alive and apologize if you've made a mistake. But if the answer is no, then let's face it, there's probably a lot of people you won't have to interact with again after high school or college. Of course, you should always be civil and kind, but if your experience together will soon be coming to a close, and you want your friendship to do the same, then you can gracefully let it go.

Your Sunny Side: Are you in a friendship that you feel stuck in? What is the best way you can handle this without sacrificing your happiness or your friend's feelings?

_____

_____

2. **Figure out what the line really means: "It's not me. It's you."** Situational conflicts are easier to resolve than personal conflicts. Maybe you disagreed with the way a friend spent their money or you're not crazy about their boyfriend. You can't control that and at the end of the day, you love your friend. But when you take offense to a part of your friend's personality or their core values, to the point that it hinders your relationship, it might be best to be honest with yourself and walk away. There are just two potential thunderstorms to take precautions for:

Thunderstorm #1: **You gossip about the person's flaws rather than telling the person directly.** This is sure to lead to flash-flooding in the friendship zone—we've all seen what Hurricane Katrina looks like in the cafeteria catfight. And the common culprit of how it always starts? Gossip. Get yourself to safety by keeping your mouth shut or by speaking with the person in a private and safe place. Remember, words don't go away and people don't usually forget them.

Thunderstorm #2: **You come off as holier-than-thou.** If you decide that you can't maintain your friendship with a person because you basically disagree with their entire life, don't say it in a way that directly displays your disapproval. It might not go over so well. Instead, be very complimentary but firm with the person so they don't feel like they are being confronted. Make it more about your personal issue with them rather than your issue with the person as a whole. Remember to isolate the problem rather than the person. Even if you think so, you don't know everything about your friend.

Your Sunny Side: Do you have a friend that you fundamentally disagree with? How do you think you can convey your feelings to the person without offending or hurting them?

_____

_____

3. Maybe your friendship just can't be salvaged—the seam is beyond repair. Sometimes there is permanent damage that can't be fixed. Occasionally, one of us may do or say something too drastic to forget. But we should all hope for that day when we want to forgive them. And while I never like to encourage holding grudges (it's not good for your own mental or physical health), sometimes, it is just too difficult to go back to the good ol' days of ice cream and root beer floats at the parlor. Even ice cream melts.

But do yourself both a favor and be cordial when you pass each other in the hallway or office. You don't have to be chums anymore, but don't put each other in the friendship slums either. Even though you may not be friends with a person any longer, it doesn't make it right for you to prevent other people from being friends with that person. You have to let each other go and live your own lives.

No one likes to call it quits with a friend. For me, it's just as bad as a break-up, if not worse. That being said, it is crucial that you get closure. Even if you never talk to the person again, it is important that you and your friend both say what you need to say in order to feel partially pacified. Keeping your hurt feelings and anger to yourself may lead to an untimely outburst. Try to keep your cool without being cold to a former friend. But no matter what, remember what you have gone through or may be going through, you're never alone.

Sunny Samples

1. Christine: "Over the past year or so, my core group of high school friends has been fracturing along fault lines due to a series of conflicts that trace back to issues that were never fully resolved in high school. Many of the conflicts are unfortunately due to the personalities of the people involved, rather than an outside conflict that might be easier to resolve. Having a fight with a close friend is one of the biggest causes of stress, especially when multiple people are involved, because friends are supposed to be the people that help you out when life gets hard. It's very difficult to be unable to turn to your friends when, in this case, they are the problem. The occasional fight is normal in most friendships, but ultimately, in a healthy friendship, a friend shouldn't be a source of stress."

2. Charlie: "I work hard to avoid conflicts with peers. Realistically, however, I think we all experience some level of conflict with others. In my experience the most effective solution is to acknowledge the issue and address it rather than trying to ignore the problem and hope it disappears. Freshmen year, one of my roommates and I initially did not get along. He was incredibly messy and careless when it came to respecting other people's belongings. Initially, I resorted to being passive/aggressive. This solved nothing. Eventually, I came to realize we couldn't read each other's minds and I had to confront him openly in a friendly, conciliatory manner. We both knew we would probably never be close friends but by the end of the year, we were able to live with each other and maybe even like each other. Just yesterday we saw each other in a campus hallway and shared a friendly conversation and a laugh."

3. Gavin: "I think conflict is an inevitable aspect of change. When people enter other stages of their life, it tends to focus their attention on new communities. At times, this can mean a movement towards college friends and a gradual fading away of high school relationships. In other instances, real life can draw you to new places and purposes. Again, this tends to distract you from past relationships. I think the key to making this process pleasant and less painful is to hold on to those relationships you treasure the most and try to incorporate them into your new life, regardless of distance or circumstance."

Zip Those Lips!

Now a word of caution if we want to salvage your friendships: *Zip the lips.* And throw away the key. They told us this as two year olds and we need it more than ever as 20-somethings. I can't stress this enough. No matter how we label it as "venting" or "complaining"—at the end of the day it's *gossiping.* And we do way too much of it.

I'm just as guilty as the rest. Hey, the first step to improvement is being honest. I should have known when my friend gave me a card for my birthday that read, "If you don't have something nice to say…come sit by me." Ouch. And it's true; gossiping can be fun—it's a way to bond. We feel an instant connection with a person as we commiserate together about a world-altering, unbelievably atrocious situation that was actually quite petty to begin with.

It's often believed that it's just women who struggle with this, but I know you guys like to gab too. Don't act so innocent boys! We've all said venomous words before, even about our best friends. The problem is—many of us never learn our lesson. The pattern is the same: when we talk about Betty to Susie who just happens to be best friends with Betty, Betty will find out. She *almost* always does. But it's the "almost" part that makes us think we can get away with it.

Gossiping is one of the greatest happiness hangovers. Unfortunately it fools us at first because it begins with an initial burst of glee, when we feel that immediate connection with someone—especially when we don't know the person very well. Afterward, though, it goes immediately downhill. When we have sold our words, there is no telling what the buyer may do with them. They may decorate it, they may damage it, or heck, they may demolish it. Just like a house. Except when you've used words instead of wood to build your house, it all falls down.

I don't know about you, but I immediately feel a sense of guilt after speaking unkindly of a person. I also feel an intense amount of anxiety knowing that I have to trust someone enough not to spill the beans like I just did. It's a terrible feeling, there's no doubt about it.

Thankfully my juicy jaw has gotten a lot tighter. And my friendships and happiness level has improved so much because of it. When we don't have to worry about our friends finding out about our hurtful comments (which we probably didn't really mean in the first place) and when we don't feel burdened by guilt, we can enjoy our friendships in a pure and wholesome way. Whether or not loose lips are something you struggle with, I hope that you'll join me in the effort to keep speak gently. We need to tread lightly when it comes to a person's integrity and character. There is always more than meets the eye, even though our mouth may try to say otherwise. We can all speak a lot kinder a lot more often.

Sunny Suggestion

Follow the trio. It's best to follow these three steps when you find yourself pinned down in a gossip trap. These nets can feel impossible to get out of but if you keep these ideas in mind, you'll be able to avert the situation without seeming judgmental or cold (which is often why we partake in gossip even when we don't want to).

1. **Don't instigate:** This is the most important step. If you have something negative to say, it's best to keep it to yourself—loose comments will lurk around and come back to haunt you if you let them out. The

more you judge others the more you will be judged in return. And if you're desperately in need to vent to someone (which I get), then talk about the issue with a person who is in no way connected to the other person you may be having an issue with. Trust is key. But as a general principle, don't bring up gossip just for the sake of gossip. One of my favorite quotes is this: "Great minds discuss ideas; average minds discuss events; small minds discuss people." Eleanor Roosevelt said that. Be a great mind like she was.

2. **Don't include yourself:** Undoubtedly there will be moments in your life (more like every day of your life) when gossip will come on the table for discussion. I've seen it at school, at work, at home—gossip is everywhere and it's another form of peer pressure tempting you to give in. As I said before, people use it as a bonding device. We love to share things we have in common with people, even when that includes a shared disliking or "hatred" of another person. Though these bonds (as you have probably learned from experience) are weak. People who establish a friendship based on a mutual enemy often become enemies themselves. It's not too long before you wonder what gossip is being said behind your back for the sake of someone else's camaraderie. So if you find yourself in the midst of mindless gossip, don't be the ringleader. And don't be a follower either. One of the most remarkable acts of bravery I've seen in a friendship was with my best friend Kelly who simply left the room when another girl came on the gossiping chopping block. That's bold—I loved it. If you have courage like that, make a stand so that people won't walk all over you. Otherwise, if it's too awkward to leave, then don't participate. It's the people who never have anything bad to say about anyone that have the most friends at the end of the day.

3. **Change the subject.** It's the festering of an unresolved conflict that's the worst part. People can get beaten to a pulp in the gossip grind. Instead of getting sucked in, redirect attention to another topic—topics that the great minds or the average minds would discuss. Current events and topics that don't include people you know can give you new insight on your *own* life, while talking about someone else's clothes won't get you anywhere. Or you could throw 'em for a loop

and actually compliment the person that was being gossiped about. Don't go with the grain when it comes to gossip.

Your Sunny Side: Do you gossip more than you should? Why do you think you do this?

_____

_____

Have you ever had an experience where your words came back to haunt you? What happened?

_____

_____

How do you think you can stop your tongue from slipping into gossip?

_____

_____

Push Away the Pressure

I learned an interesting idea in middle school and I've kept it with me ever since. 10% of people will adore you, 10% of people aren't going to like you much, and the rest, that 80%, is in the middle. Your behavior and demeanor can sway them one-way or the other. For many of us, it is this "middle" section that we tend to worry about—what people think of our clothes, our hair, our personality—the list goes on. Thankfully it lessens with age, but peer approval can detract a great amount of happiness if we're not careful.

When we are constantly fretting about how we come off to the world, whether it is toward our friends, strangers, acquaintances, or enemies, we are worrying more about how to please others then how to please ourselves. And while it is important to value esteemed opinions, unnecessary opinions shouldn't define our self-worth. We have to remember to stay true to ourselves. Our friends can help us keep that sense of truth, especially when we're challenged by peer pressure.

Sunny Samples

1. Colby: "The approval of my friends matters very much as I know they are quality people, for whom I have great respect. While peers in general still matter (I think that's only human), I am finally growing enough in confidence and strength to be comfortable with myself."

2. Christina: "I'm not a huge drinker, but I still love to go out and have fun. It really bugs me when I feel weird pressure to drink or I feel like someone is making me feel bad for not liking to drink. I don't really get the fun in forcing someone who hates drinking to take a shot with you...I guess that is something I've never understood. Usually I can just brush it off, but sometimes the weird pressure I feel really gets on my nerves."

3. Collin: "I have experienced peer pressure in many different forms. I have been pressured to take drugs, fight, steal cars, money, bikes, cheat, and behave and dress a certain way. I have submitted to it on occasion and ignored it on others. In general, I would say that submitting to peer pressure regardless of the type is always the wrong choice for your happiness. While you may elect to pursue the course of action your peers are pressuring you to take, you should arrive at it by yourself. While you might consider your peers' input, it is ultimately your life. Deciding your fate for yourself is part of the process of maturing into a confident and happy person."

4. Ashley: "In all the times I have experienced peer pressure I have found that it is subtle yet strong. So strong that most of the time it is easier to just go along with the pressure than fight it. I feel happier that the pressure is gone, but at the same time, much less happy because I gave into it.

However when I do resist the pressure, I feel good about myself because I stood up for my beliefs and I resisted."

5. Jessica: "While it can be uncomfortable at first, I find that people are fairly respectful once it becomes clear that I am not willing to compromise myself. Honestly, if someone isn't willing to respect your personal values, then they aren't your friend."

Standing up for what you believe in takes a lot of courage. People often take personal offense when you deliberately choose not to make the same choices they make. And, because of it, you may even lose a friend or two. I know I have. Yet I have never regretted those decisions. There is great happiness to be had in knowing that you are strong enough to walk your own walk instead of trying to talk someone else's talk. I have found that ultimately, people will respect you for the choices that *you* decide to make, not for the choices made when you caved in.

Sunny Suggestions

1. Phone a friend. You always have a lifeline—especially with smart phones galore. Call a friend, a parent—heck, I called my grandma when I needed to get out of a tricky situation. You don't have to feel embarrassed for not joining in. Often people are so caught up in their own world they probably won't notice if you just quietly excuse yourself. You don't need to make a scene when you stand up to an uncomfortable situation. Just walk away.

Your Sunny Side: Next time you're in an awkward position, who can you count on to save the day and how will you remove yourself from the situation?

2. Be cool in another way. I remember hearing about a boy in high school who would drink out of a milk carton instead of drinking beer, and "the trend" caught on like wildfire. People may think it's cool to party or drink but you can be even cooler by doing something out of the ordinary. Also, who cares what's in a sprite or a coke? No one knows anyway, especially if they have been drinking. Drink what you want, do what you want. Don't let people force you to do anything you don't already want to do.

Your Sunny Side: What can you do that's different when you're at a party and you don't feel like drinking or smoking?

_____

_____

3. Find something else to do. Quite frankly I have much more fun going out to dinner with my girlfriends or watching a movie together in our pj's. Memories are so much better when you can remember them the next day. Plus, you need to ask yourself—am I with the right friends if we don't want to do the same things together? With high school and college, people can change so much in a short period of time; it's understandable if your interests start to separate. Just because you don't want to stay out drinking every night with your friend—if you firmly state that you chose not to, she can't drag you along.

Your Sunny Side: What do you actually enjoy doing with your friends? Are your interests in alignment? What can you do that you enjoy besides partying together?

_____

_____

_____

I hope that no matter where you are in your life, you will have friends that love you for who you are. I hope that they will respect the choices that you make for yourself and I hope you will let your friends make their own choices for themselves. Of course, if you think your friend is making a grave decision you should step in, but remember, you need to respect rational people who make reasonable decisions, even if those choices are different from yours.

Various friends will come and go throughout our lives and I hope you will make an honest effort to keep them ever in your heart if you make each other happy. I know it can be easy to let the familiar faces fade with the years, but keep the sun shining on your friends. Share your light with each other.

Back in the Saddle Again

We meet new people on a constant basis—especially when you make a life change, like college. Starting back at the kindergarten stage of friendship isn't always easy. It can be awkward when you get the, "So what's your major?" type questions or the getting-to-know-you play dates for coffee or shopping that encourage a hopeful friendship. But we're young adults, not elementary school kids. Here's the good news: the closer we are with a friend, the happier we'll feel.

Even if you are the type to make fast friends, we all take time to really open ourselves up to a meaningful friendship that is based not only on inside jokes and silly games, but also on trust and loyalty. Instead of being passive about potential friendships, we need to reach out and be open to new possibilities—to new forms of happiness. You can't expect others to always initiate. Of course, it takes two to tango, but when you make an effort to be welcoming and kind, people will naturally be drawn to you. Being friendly gets you friends! (What a concept!) I know it sounds elementary, but sometimes it's easier said than done. So put that grin on your face and smile like you mean it. You're much more likely to make a friend if you're friendly in the first place.

In all actuality though, people are not overtly friendly with one another. This can make potential friendships fumble. Think about it—haven't you walked to class before and even though you've seen a certain person for the past five years, you still don't say "hi" to them, or even acknowledge their presence? In fact, many people will often avert their gaze if you try to make eye contact them—don't dare send them a smile now, they might run away! In fact, we're often surprised if a stranger smiles at us or if someone we've never met talks to us. Everyone has learned to keep to themselves—but are we happier for it? I don't think so. Even though not everyone will become your best friend, it's important to be friendly with everyone. Even when someone denies your smile, smile anyway.

I know, when meeting people, I can be shy at first. It takes me a long time to really form a close bond. I've definitely been guilty of closing myself off in certain social situations because I was afraid I would say something stupid or because I thought another person wouldn't like me. But then I realized, what do I have to lose? So what if they don't like me—there are plenty of other fish in the sea that just might. You could be losing out on a lot of great potential friends if you never get the nerve to introduce yourself to them. So when you're out and about, smile at people, ask them how they're doing (genuinely—not just as a polite nicety), and make yourself more vulnerable to valuable friendships. Closing yourself off just keeps people away.

Sunny Samples

1.   Heather: "In my junior year of college, I spent one semester in Missouri as an international exchange student. Coming from France, I had many challenges to overcome, including making new friends. Although I was trying my best to be social and open-minded, I have always been reserved and shy. However, by making some effort, I became part of an awesome group of students that were mostly international and we were all new to the same town. We became closer by sharing the same fears and overcoming the same challenges. After becoming more confident, I also started making American friends. I am still in touch with them now and I can say that it was one of the best semesters in my life. I have found that the more difficult the challenge, the more rewarding the outcome."

2. Melanie: "When I started college, I knew that I wanted to make really great friends really quickly. I thought that was an unrealistic expectation, but I also didn't realize that nearly every other freshman at UCLA wanted the exact same thing. During my first week, I was a little more outgoing than I would normally be and I never rejected a social invitation. The next thing I knew, I had a bunch of new friends! Making friends is easy for me, but making deep, lasting friendships is tougher. New friends always make me happy. However, I can feel dissatisfied when I have had friends for a few months and those friendships are not progressing to deeper levels. I would rather have a handful of friends who I can both trust and have fun with, than dozens of friends who I only go to parties with."

3. Lynn: "Anytime I have taken a risk and entered new friendships they result in greater happiness in my life. I think putting yourself out there and meeting new people and letting people in is a risk, but it is always rewarding when they too let you in and together you form a bond."

Sunny Suggestion

Be brave: You have nothing to lose when you introduce yourself to someone. More than likely, they will be grateful that someone wants to talk to them. Besides, anyone who is so self-important to not value a friendly conversation isn't worth any more of your time anyway. I know I always feel proud of myself for taking these little "social risks" that have a huge payoff. When I miss that chance to say hello to someone—when I just sit there silently—I always regret it.

Your Sunny Side: How open are you when meeting new people? How do you think this might affect your friendships?

If you want to be a happier person, then spread joy and love wherever you go. Don't keep it to yourself. Be a friend to a person when no one else will be. Be patient. Reserve judgment. Love your friends for the people they are—for their flaws, for their idiosyncrasies, and most importantly, for the things that make them so amazing. Our friends are the sunshine of our lives and we have to help them shine. Be a light to them in return and you're bound to get that golden California glow.

I leave you with a quote from my favorite president, Abraham Lincoln:

"The better part of one's life consists of his friendships."

A Happy
Family Tree

Unlike the friends that we chose, we are born into a family. Who's to say why we end up where we do. And while we can't control if we're born in the hood, a humble home, or the Hollywood hills—it's all about our reaction to these circumstances. No matter who raises us, it is our choice as to how we respond. I won't deny the power of genetics or the way you've been raised, but at the end of the day, you decide to be a victim or a survivor of your circumstances. Having a great family is a wonderful blessing but not everyone is blessed at birth with loving parents and a happy home. Life is not always fair—your family may be your first experience of that. Some are born into mansions with nannies and a personal chef. Others are born in a tattered hut with no clean water. And many of us are in the middle. We all have our good days and bad days despite who our family is or where we are located. It's what we do with those days that matter.

It's not easy to make universal maxims for families. Perhaps your family is your greatest source of happiness. Or maybe your family is your greatest source of pain. Perhaps both. Unlike our friends, our goals, and our spirituality, which is ultimately our choosing, our family is given to us—for better or for worse. And while our happiness should be internal, the people that surround us can have a great effect on our general demeanor. Our parents are the first examples we have in life and we learn many lessons from them, both good and bad. No parents are perfect but most parents try to give us their best. No matter what your parents were like while you were growing up, the family dynamic has a great effect on our life values. Yet ultimately it is our decision as to how we want to apply those values to our own lives. Here's how some of you see it.

Sunny Samples

1.   Tara: "My parents have been the most influential people in my life. My parents are honest, hardworking, kind, loving people and I try to be more like them every day. I love them and I am so thankful for the standards, morals, and values they have taught me to abide by. The values I have, thanks to them, allow me to live the kind of life that makes it a little easier to find happiness."

2.   Peter: "My parents have been the most important people in shaping my values. I am so thankful that they have helped me make the right decisions in life. They've been the greatest role models and while I sometimes disagreed with their decisions when I was younger, I now appreciate most of their choices."

3.   Derek: "The values my dad instilled in me have shown me that family is the most important thing in your life and you should do anything and everything to keep them your top priority."

4.   Sean: "My parents are 100% responsible for shaping all of my values, for teaching me right from wrong, for teaching me how to be a responsible adult, for teaching me to work hard, stay focused, and to stay true to myself. I like to think that my parents taught me to work for money to buy my own things instead of their giving me everything. Even though it would be nice to have everything handed to me, the feeling of success and self-satisfaction that I get by earning my own living definitely makes me a much happier person."

5.   Dillon: "My dad is a deadbeat. He is a meth addict and a drug dealer who has been in and out of jail and prison. For a really long time, I felt ethically bound to him, as if I was somehow responsible for paying for his crimes and was doomed to fail because of him. This made me incredibly and predictably unhappy. I was unmotivated until I learned how to deal

with it. I did most of my 'growing up' on my own terms and refused to view my parents as role models."

Sunny Suggestions

In college I took a developmental psychology course and one thing I really appreciated from the class was the distinction of the four kinds of parenting and how each one affects their children's lives differently. The good news is that no matter how you were raised, you can still get a hold of your happiness. It all comes back to the perspective you choose. The four types of parents are listed below—find your match and more importantly, find out how to be happy regardless of the type of family you have.

1. Your Sunny Side: You have authoritative parents. These parents are clear communicators with their children. They believe in fairness and reciprocity. They allow their child reasonable autonomy as the child matures and they are attentive to their child's needs. These kids often turn out high in self-esteem with a positive and optimistic demeanor.
_____ Does this sound like you? If you're in this boat, stay in it! The water is nice—we're talking Bahamas status. You're a natural for happiness and your parents' love, encouragement, and stability has helped you grow into a confident person. Be grateful for the gift of your parents and give back to them and others with a friendly demeanor.

2. Your Sunny Side: You have authoritarian parents. Everything in this home is a no-questions asked policy. Do as they say, not as they do. If you ever make a mistake, don't expect to be quickly forgiven and you'd better do what they expect of you—or else. These parents are strict, no ifs, ands, or buts about it. Their children often have trouble with building up their self-esteem and they may seek drugs or alcohol or misbehavior in general to rebel against the tight leash that's been strapped on. It's hard to be friendly when you feel like you'll get shut down all the time.
_____ Does this sound like you? It might be harder to learn that others won't withdraw love whenever you make a mistake; but there are people out

there who will love you, mistakes and all. Try and surround yourself with these kinds of people—people who make smart decisions while expressing compassion. You're in need for some extra TLC. No one has a right to take that away from you, especially not your parents. If they won't support what makes you happy, then surround yourself with people who will.

3. Your Sunny Side: You have permissive parents. These parents let you stay up all night, let you do poorly in school, in fact, they'll let you do anything, whether you ask for permission or not. Sure, they love you, but they also let you off too easily and while this may seem "cool" in the short term, it doesn't pay off in the long run. You may be momentarily happy when you get that easy "yes," but when all your friends go to college and you can't because you were never encouraged to pursue your academics, it might not feel so good. These kids often lack the motivation they need to succeed because their parents didn't teach them what hard work and dedication looked like. Their parents don't expect much of them so they learn not to expect much of themselves.

_____ Does this sound like you? Thankfully, it's never too late to whip yourself into shape. You need a little extra motivation, but your happiness is quick to follow suit once you've got your determination in drive. Even if your parents don't hold you to high standards you shouldn't sell yourself short. You deserve the best chance—and being complacent is not the answer. Reach higher and your happiness will also get off the ground.

4. Your Sunny Side: You have disengaged parents. These parents could care less what you do. They're often so busy in their own world that they hardly notice you. They don't seem to have an opinion no matter what you do, let alone knowing where you are. Their children are often abused or neglected, never experiencing love, discipline, or for that matter, any attention. This type of parenting barely resembles a relationship and often leaves the child feeling very lost.

_____ Does this sound like you? It may be hard to recover from parenting like this but it's important that you find role models or caretakers who can show you what a real familial relationship is made of. You deserve to experience love, happiness, and meaningful relationships. Even though you may not have had a fair start, it doesn't mean that you can't still make it right later in life. Someone is willing to fight for you; you just have to be willing to fight for the life you want.

No matter what type of family you've found yourself in, there can always be a sunny side. If nothing else, it may be realizing that a family is meant to serve as a foundation, not a fortress. Your family is what you make of it—you may love your family dearly or perhaps you desperately can't wait to get away. Either way it's a reciprocal relationship and both parties, you, your parents and surrounding family members, are all affected by the choices all of you make. While you can't choose your family, you can choose your mentality and I hope that you'll make happiness, kindness, and love a part of the legacy that you'll leave within your family, even if you leave that family behind someday.

The Picket Fence that's Peeling

Let's be real, the "Leave it to Beaver" family is almost non-existent nowadays. Children are raised by grandparents, single mothers, single fathers, siblings, foster care, two men, two women, or friends—just to name a few. The "traditional" family of the mother and father duo is no longer the norm. But more important than a bloodline, having positive role models means more than any genetic relation ever could. As young adults we need someone who can be there to love, guide and support us. We need figures in our lives that will not only challenge us to take the higher road, but who will also laugh with us and love us for who we are.

If that person happens to be your mother or your father, give thanks. And if that person is a grandparent, an aunt, an uncle, a sibling, or a friend, give thanks for them as well. Be glad you have someone in your life that is willing and wanting to take care of you. It's a big deal. Rather than wallowing in self-pity because you have a less than "perfect" family (sans the white picket fence and golden retriever), appreciate the family that you've been given—even the beautiful homes can have peeling paint on the inside.

The Mentors that Matter Most

When you look back on your childhood, who made the difference? Who took the time to love you, protect you, and care for you the way that all children should be? I have two influential people in my life (other than my parents) who have made all the difference in my world. I wouldn't be who I am today if it weren't for their dedication to my upbringing.

The first is my Auntie Nette. How she got that name, I'll never know. She's my mom's sister and I'll never forget how she loved me as a child and how she loves me now as young woman. Her love has been unconditional—always. From rocking me to sleep to taking me to church, my Auntie Nette made life something to cherish. I was only two when my mother was diagnosed with breast cancer and I remember my Auntie Nette taking care of me so many nights. When I would ask questions about my mom's condition, she would have the perfect answer so that I wouldn't worry. She shielded me from so much, but she also taught me so much. She was the first to introduce me to country music and to the wonderful combination of mashed potatoes, chicken and corn. More importantly, she taught me about having faith and dedication toward family. Also about selfless love, compassion, and patience. I still talk to her every day and we never miss an opportunity to tell each other that we love each other. I love you, Auntie Nette. (Told you I never miss the chance!)

The second mentor is my Grandma Joan. As a fellow Bruin, she is my hero. My grandma embodies grace, patience, and virtue. She has never said a foul word about anyone (I wish I could say the same—and I've had my mouth washed out with soap to prove it). She is creative, intelligent (she does a New York Times crossword puzzle every day), and I love it when she laughs. She taught me how to cross-stitch and she makes a mean peanut butter and jelly sandwich. Don't even get me started on our See's Candy tradition. From kindergarten to tenth grade, she would pick me up every Friday after school and take me out for a Baskin Robbin's scoop of bubblegum ice cream or a Noah's bagel with extra cream cheese. As a college student, she sent me care packages, and whenever I'm home we go out for our regular Friday night dinners. I especially love the summer with Grammy J (as I jokingly call her, or Joanie when I really want to make her flinch). Every summer she rents a beach house for two weeks for the entire family—where we inevitably goad Grandma Joan to dip her feet into the water at least once. It's usually quite a feat. No pun intended. But best of all, she loves family more than anything and she's made me have that same love for my family.

Of course, my parents mean the world to me. Somehow, when I arrived on February 13, 1991, the stork decided to drop me off on the best doorstep anyone could ever hope for.

My dad is a comedic genius. He is an impromptu songwriter, and bursts out the original lyrics to artists like Lady Gaga. My dad got my Grandma Joan's genius genes and he motivates me to think harder, try again, and do better on a daily basis. My dad is what happiness looks like with his perky haircut, his grandiose hand gestures and his hopeful heart. More than anything, I love dancing with my dad. From the Lion King airlifts as a preschooler to the Debutante Ball waltz as a senior in high school, my dad always sweeps me off my feet. Everyone has a different relationship with their father. I've always been my dad's "Little Princess" and he's always been "Unforgettable" to me (yes, we sing the Nat King Cole and Natalie Cole duet on a frequent basis). Here's what you had to say about your dads and how they added to your happiness.

Sunny Samples

1. Peter: "My relationship with my dad is one of the strongest in my life. I look up to him more than anyone. It makes me happy to know that he has been so instrumental in helping me become who I am today. He gives me the best advice whether it is about school, relationships, or friends, and when I give my friends advice, I always find myself referring back to things he's told me."

2. Liz: "My father and I are not very close, although we used to be. All we do is argue, and he always assumes I'm making the wrong choices in my life. I feel like nothing I do is ever good enough for him. He is very strict and old fashioned and embarrasses me often. This affects my happiness, because I really do wish I were one of those girls who is super close with their dad. I miss that."

3. Steven: "My relationship with my father was not that great while I was growing up. He was pushing me to be the typical heterosexual male that plays football and watches women's beach volleyball. However, much to my surprise, once I 'came out,' our relationship grew considerably. I like having a father that is supportive, so my happiness has definitely improved."

4. Dylan: "My relationship with my dad is amazing. Without him I honestly doubt I would ever be happy. He is one of the few people I could call at ANY time and tell him whatever I want, and I know he can make me feel better because he believes in me."

5. Bristol: "My father's support from a young age is the reason I have self-confidence and the happiness that comes with loving who you are. Every day of my life, my father told me that I am smart, beautiful, and have limitless potential. I have grown up believing this is so. My dad's continuous presence in my life has given me more happiness than any present, nanny, or toy could have ever given me, and I am so grateful for every sacrifice he made so that I could understand the difference between material happiness and genuine personal satisfaction."

Sunny Suggestion

Be a dear to dad. No matter what your relationship is like with your father, I hope that you'll be able to bring out the best in each other. Sometimes our dads can get the least love in the family, so make sure your dad feels special by going on fun outings or having nice chats every now and then. I call my dad on a regular basis just to let him know that I love him. It also helps to find a niche with your dad—when you two have a shared passion, like a love of sports, books, or movies, you'll always have a point of relation, even when the rest of your relationship feels rocky.

Your Sunny Side: What is your relationship like with your father?

_____

_____

_____

What are some of your happiest memories with him?

_____

_____

_____

How can you improve your relationship with your dad?

_____

_____

_____

There's nothing like a mother's love.

My mom is the perfect match for my dad and me. She's one of the most enthusiastic people I know and she is my biggest fan, even when there's not much to cheer about. At least once a month (whenever anything exciting happens) I see the "Marila Cook dance." She supports me in every endeavor, from playing the piano to writing this book and I support her with all of her pursuits—from nursing, to volunteering, to counseling. Simply put, she is brilliant. She has her M.S.N. in nursing and for the past thirty years, she has been treating patients in critical care and the operating room. No matter whom she meets, she loves every person in some way and I'm thankful to say that I'm included in that line-up. Not to mention, she makes a mean macaroni and cheese. To top it off, her cake baking and decorating skills are Martha Stewart magazine cover- worthy.

More than just my mom's dedication to our "Cook" family name or her patients, my mom is one of the most compassionate people I have ever known. She is generous in every way and gives so much of herself, no matter what she is doing. I love her so much.

Here's what you had to say about your moms.

Sunny Samples

1. Jamie: "My mom knows everything, and I mean *everything*. I love hanging out with my mom because I look up to her a lot. We have a great relationship, but at the same time we are so similar that we can butt heads. We get in heated arguments occasionally, but they always end in tearful apologies and ice cream. Being able to talk to my mom about anything makes me really happy."

2. Justin: "My mom is unsuccessful, but she has always been incredibly caring to me and has always tried hard to give me the best she could. She is incredibly unlucky, and it took me a long time to realize this, so for a while I thought her failures were due to *her* being a failure. I have re-established a relationship with her recently that I was unwilling to maintain before and this has been emotionally uplifting for me."

3. Lisa: "My relationship with my mom always seems to change. She will try to be my 'friend' and get information about my personal life from me, but then she tells other people. She has violated my trust, and now I hardly tell her anything. She is very critical, always commenting on my weight and appearance. I think her attitude comes from her self-esteem issues. This affects my happiness because the negative things she says change the way I feel about myself."

4. Erica: "My mom has always been and always will be my best friend. After my father left and before my mom remarried, it was just she and I because I'm an only child. My relationship with my mom makes me happy because I love that we're so close, but I incessantly worry about her health, safety, and happiness which isn't so fun."

5. Anna: "My mom's love is truly irreplaceable. So when my mom and I had a major falling out over family issues, I felt a void in my life that could not be filled by a hectic school schedule, a boyfriend, volunteering, and supportive friends. It wasn't until my mom and I had repaired our relationship that I felt back to myself and regained a more steady level of happiness."

Sunny Suggestion

Make every day Mother's Day. If you can, give your mom a hug today. Or give her a call. Most mothers care deeply about their children and they want nothing but their little one's happiness (let's face it, you'll always be their "baby"). Give your mom some happiness by reaching out to her rather than running away. She brought you into this world so bring her back some joy as a way to thank her for giving you the gift of life.

Your Sunny Side: What is your relationship like with your mom?

_____

_____

_____

What are some of your happiest memories with her?

_____

_____

_____

What can you do to improve your relationship with your mom?

_____

_____

_____

Till Death Do Us Part

I don't have siblings. I guess the stork was flying solo that day and didn't want to go back to baby island ever again. Frankly, I don't mind his decision—I've been happy with what I've had, since that's all I've ever known. Growing up, I loved it. I didn't have to share Barbies, I got all of my parent's attention, and I never had peas and carrots thrown at my face. I recently realized that my case is pretty rare; I am one out of ten kids, on average, that doesn't have siblings.

I'm not regretful that I don't have a brother or a sister. But I recently learned that people who have siblings often have an upper hand, especially when it comes to happiness. They are quicker to learn "theories of mind," realizing that other people have beliefs, knowledge, and desires that are different from their own. It's the notion that we all find happiness in our own way. Siblings help us learn how to understand people more efficiently—we have a greater appreciation for what makes other people happy, not just ourselves.

Also, siblings teach us valuable lessons about the relationships we will have later in life. Considering your relationship with your sibling is the longest relationship you'll probably ever have, there's a lot of prep work we can do with our siblings before we someday have other relationships. At first it may not come easy being with siblings but the investment can be worth the wait. While similarity and the 'mere exposure effect' suggest that the more time you spend with a person, the more likely you'll like them—this is not always the case when it comes to your genetic counterparts. Often, in the beginning, sibling relationships are rife with conflict. I've seen it all— the screaming, the hair pulling, the tattle tales and the troublemakers. This can be a great source of unhappiness for kidlets but thankfully many sibling relationships improve with time—hair grows back and the bond rebuilds. Here's how you think your siblings contributed to your happiness.

Sunny Samples

1. Jill: "I have two younger brothers. One is 4 years younger than me and the other is 11 years younger than me. Brian (age 14) is pretty much my best

friend. I can tell him anything and he will never judge me nor betray my trust. Brandon (age 7) is a little monster. I love him to death, but he is your typical 'tattle tale' and it annoys me. But I guess all little kids are that way, right? I love my brothers and they always make me happy when I'm feeling low."

2. Devon: "I have an older sister. I would not be half as mature as I am now if it weren't for her. I also have a younger brother that I helped raise because my mom had him with my stepdad when I was about 10. My little brother is a key to my happiness because he looks up to me and just seeing how big he smiles or how hard he tries when I come to his sporting events warms my heart."

3. Claire: "I'm an only child. I mostly like it because I get a lot of attention, but sometimes I think it would be nice to have someone around my own age to get advice from and to give advice to. Also, coming to college and constantly being surrounded by people, even in my own room, is something that I had to get used to. There are several things that I've noticed that set me apart from those who have siblings, but ultimately, I enjoy being an only child. Though I want to have a lot of kids!"

Sunny Suggestion

So whether you're riding solo or you're living in your own Octomom ordeal, learn what you can from your siblings. Make your sibling feel special by having little sayings or little adventures that make your bond unique. Give each other the gift of happiness rather than the curse of conflict. It'll be a blessing both for you and your family.

Your Sunny Side: If you have a sibling, what's your relationship like with them? If you don't have a sibling, how do you feel about being an only child?

How does your sibling(s) or your solo situation add to your happiness?

_____

_____

What are three ways you can improve your relationship with your sibling(s) so that each of you can get more out of the relationship?

1. _____

2. _____

3. _____

Pet Pals

Of course, I have to share my ideas about pets. Maybe because I am an only child my cat is like my brother, but regardless of how many siblings you have, a pet can be a tremendous source of happiness. I figure it is only fitting to talk about pets under the family chapter because as far as I'm concerned, they are part of the family.

Kiko is my pride and joy. He is a Chocolate Point, Applehead Siamese cat although he seems to think he is a panther prowling the house and we are merely the prey to abide by his biddings. He does everything with us—he sits on the counter while we eat dinner (I know, I know—my poor mother can't stand it), he sits along the edge of the bathtub while I take a bubble bath, dipping his tail in, and he even sleeps under the covers with me, resting his head on the pillow. Some of you might find this abominable but I find it simply adorable. Even as I write this, he is curled up in a ball by my feet.

Pets are an essential component to happiness because, most of the time, they express unconditional love. They remind us to just relax—to take a nap or two, and to see the simple joys of life—like a good meal, a good cuddle, a good rest. These sweet creatures show us that it's the little comforts in life that can truly matter.

Multiple studies have shown that there really may be something to man's best friend. In 1990, Siegel found that elderly people who have dogs are less likely to visit doctors frequently and they are more likely to survive heart attacks. There are lasting benefits to keeping a pet. Whether it is your beloved bulldog, your hearty hermit crab (hey, I've had one and those things live a long time), or your lazy lizard—animals are entertaining, charming, and somewhat helpless without us. It's rewarding to know that we can not only keep something alive, but that we can love them and take care of them so that they can enjoy their own happiness. Here's what you shared about your pets.

Sunny Samples

1. Erin: "I have two dogs and have always had several pets growing up. I would get in trouble for keeping animals in my closet in high school—guinea pigs, hamsters, a mouse, a rat, a bearded dragon. I love animals and I definitely think they make me a happier person. They don't judge, they always have time to hang out, and they love you unconditionally. What's better than that?!"

2. Sam: "I love laying on my bed with my two cats. They're always glad to see me when I walk through the door. I'd be so lonely without them because they hang out with me after my parents have gone to bed. Even though they're not people, they make good company."

3. Kenna: "My life would not be nearly as happy without my puppy, Torri. There's something to be said about having an adorable, reliable face run to you once you get home from school. They're so excited to see you and you can't help but melt. My golden retriever is amazing. She's the biggest sweetheart and the most amazing dog on the planet. The companionship someone can have with a pet is indescribable and that's exactly what I have with Torri. I love her to death."

Sunny Suggestion

A relationship with an animal is really what you make of it--you get back what you put in. If you want to have a strong bond with your pet, then you have to make an effort. Feed them, take them for walks (if they're a dog or a horse—that might not go over so well with a cat), and make sure they're comfortable. More than anything, take time to pet them, talk kindly to them, and check in with them whenever you're at home. Happiness is almost surely guaranteed when you keep your animals happy.

Your Sunny Side: If you have a pet, how do they add to your happiness?

_____

_____

Home is Where Your Heart Is

Even as we grow up, the important thing is that we still search for happiness at home. A common myth is that teenagers are only trouble for their parents and that the relationship can be quick to crumble. It doesn't have to be this way. I believe that it is a parent's responsibility to be supportive rather than condescending during our journeys of self-discovery that we all need to go on. More than anything, no matter how old we are, we need to feel loved by our parents or those who have mentored us.

The only problem is that parents can sometimes forget *how* we need to be loved. They learned how to love us when we were children; they had 13 years of practice. But love evolves with age and parents can have a hard time relating to the problems young adults may be facing today. Each new generation has its own set of challenges and circumstances to concur. Some problems never change but many of them evolve. So even if they remember those years like they were yesterday, the times are certainly a-changin' and so are the problems we are facing.

At the same time, we shouldn't put our parents through the ringer. We need to remember that there are consequences to our choices that not only we, but our parents, often have to face. Our parents just want to keep us safe—they want to protect us (not just physically, but our hearts and reputations as well). When we remember that their guidance is done out of love rather than malice, we can have a much better understanding of where they are coming from. Chances are, you'll thank them later. Looking back I'm grateful for what my parents did for me, even if I didn't appreciate their decisions when I was a teenager.

I know my dad struggled with me growing up. When he couldn't tickle me anymore or call me "Laurnie Bug," he didn't take it too well (even though he still does both). And when I got a boyfriend, that's when it really got hard. Whether or not you were "Daddy's Little Girl" or the "Like Father, Like Son," it can be hard for our parents when they watch us develop our independence. Within reason, we have to make our own mistakes and learn for ourselves. While our parents ultimately want us to become self-sufficient (no one wants their thirty year old son still waking up to mommy's smiley face pancakes), sometimes it's still not easy for our parents to let us go.

Perhaps the hardest part is when our parents have to watch us make our own choices. Especially when those choices could or *will* become mistakes. And much of the time, it's because our parents have made those same mistakes when they were our age and they can foresee the consequences better than we can. Yet we need to learn how to make decisions, in the moment, without our mommies and daddies holding our hands and telling us what to do. That's just part of growing up and when our parents prevent us from this for fear that we'll fall down, we'll never learn how to pick ourselves back up again on our own. I believe that a good parent is one that prevents us with caution, guards us within reason, and has patience with us as we learn.

With each passing year, we gain more perspective, more knowledge, and more responsibility--and ideally, we gain more happiness. A good life is one in which we can look back on our past, see the mistakes that we made, and know that we learned from these choices to make a better life for ourselves and for future generations.

Our relationship with our parents is constantly evolving, and I think that it is a parent's job to remember and respect that. A love for a three year old or a ten year old is not the same kind of love that a fourteen year old or a twenty year old needs. But, nonetheless, it is still love. The best kind of love is mutual, no matter how old. Here are your thoughts.

Sunny Samples

1. Paul: "We have all definitely grown closer as I've gotten older. I can now talk to my parents about things that I never could when I was younger. The dynamic has changed so much from just being under their control as a child to really understanding and appreciating the role they have played in my life as an adult."

2. Tiffany: "For as long as I can remember I would have long talks with my parents about life and the struggles I was having and they would always be there for me. I think that now that I am a bit older (and hopefully a bit wiser) I have a little more perspective on life and it is easier for me to see why I should do what my parents tell me. During my younger years, it was difficult for me to understand why they wanted me to be home at a certain time or did not want me to spend all of my money at the mall. But now I see how their counsel has benefited my overall well-being. I am grateful that they loved me unconditionally."

3. Liam: "I guess my relationship with my parents has changed from a teacher/mentor role to a friend role. As a child I viewed my parents as the law. Now I view my parents more as friends."

4. Kelsey: "The only change within my family is that I'm finally at a place where I can relate to them and have serious conversations. They have always loved me and been there for me. Now I love the fact that we can laugh and have a good time as adults but still have that parent-child bond."

5. Brianna: "They still treat me like a little girl living in their house and I still look at them with awe and respect. Until I move away and start paying for all my own things, I don't think our views of each other will change. We've had little quarrels here and there, but we'll always be close."

Sunny Suggestion

Appreciate change. With each passing year there is something new to enjoy from your relationship with your parents. When you were a kid perhaps you loved going to the park with your parents. Now, as you get older, you appreciate a good heart to heart talk with your mom or going out to dinner with both of them. Time changes our relationships as we become more independent but it doesn't mean that it has to change for the worse. Let the years of your relationship with your family build a stronger bond.

Your Sunny Side: As a child, how did your relationship with your family add to your happiness?

_____

_____

How does your current relationship with your family affect your happiness?

_____

_____

Don't Be a Beauty School Drop Out

One of my favorite laughable quotes is from Frenchie in *Grease*: "Beauty is pain." I think the same can go for our relationship with our parents. Sometimes it takes a few struggles before we can develop a stronger and more "beautiful" relationship with our parents. It is often assumed that young adults fight with their parents more during their teenage years than at any other time. Whether or not this is true, what is more important than the conflicts themselves is the *way* in which we resolve these conflicts. Arguments are inevitable—people are bound to disagree. Different perspectives and different life experiences lead to different opinions. But as I said before, rather than being a victim of your circumstances, be a survivor of your situation. Take the higher road. Depending on your personal situation, this may include apologizing, removing yourself, or agreeing to disagree. Just because you are the "child" of your parents does not mean you still have to act like one when you have a fight with them.

I definitely had my fair share of arguments when I became a teenager. While there have been moments when I or my parents have lost our cool, we always do our best to utilize self-control. The more heated the fight, the longer everyone's happiness is put off. It's wasted time in my opinion. The harder part is finding forgiveness. While anger can be momentary, the pain and sadness after-effects can be long term if we hold on to them too tightly. It can be easier to keep a grudge than to process the emotional impact of a fight and then let it go. But if you hold a grudge you'll go numb. Numb to anger, numb to sadness, and numb to happiness. You never want this. That's why it's so important that, during familial conflict, we forgive and ask for forgiveness. Your family can be one of your greatest sources of joy but if you're hung up on your anger, you're only denying yourself an emotionally happy life. After you've given yourself the time you need to recover from being upset, look for the good and don't dwell on the pain.

What choice will you make when it comes to responding to familial conflict? Will you respond with anger, apathy, or peace? It's your decision and yours alone. I hope you'll choose peace over pessimism and optimism over outrage.

Sunny Samples

1. Peter: "I don't really have many conflicts with my parents anymore. When we do disagree, I'm now at a point of maturity where we can discuss things rationally instead of getting angry with each other. The quality of our relationship is a big part of what makes me so happy."
2. Jennifer: "Though I have rarely had conflict with my parents, when I do, it strongly affects my happiness. Getting in an argument with my parents changes the entire mood in our house, and affects the entire family. When one relationship is disturbed it affects all the others. Conflict with

my parents makes me unhappy because I often feel like something was blown out of proportion, and that I should have just let something go. That feeling of regret is frustrating. Thankfully, my parents are understanding and we resolve our problems quickly."

3. Jake: "Well, my dad was very abusive. But it didn't take long for me to become tough enough to fight back, so that was how the majority of our conflicts were resolved. My mom and I disagree on a lot of issues (she is really into alternative medicine and that infuriates me), but we have learned to disagree and give each other space on our issues."

4. Chloe: "I'm an only child so I grew up very, very close to my parents (and I still am!). Even though we bicker constantly, when we're actually mad about something it makes me feel SUPER uncomfortable. We don't really get into conflicts that easily. Something that can really affect my happiness is when my dad makes comments about my eating or exercise habits or even my weight. I know I'm not the skinniest girl in the world, and my dad has issues of his own about eating that I think he sometimes projects on me. I know that he has my best interest in mind, but his comments about me eating too much and not exercising enough (I work out like 4 times a week!) can really get to me. I think he has this weird fear that he's going to have some overweight daughter and that's going to make life really hard for me and he just wants me to be as happy as possible."

5. Louise: "I was fortunate to grow up in a household where my parents rarely fought. Any potential argument was quickly settled because my parents tried to understand each other and reach an agreement. From observing my parents, I learned that when I had a conflict with someone, I needed to compromise and understand the other person's point of view. Tackling arguments in a rational manner, rather than yelling and bickering, allows me to be happier."

Sunny Suggestions

1. Don't say it to my face. My Grandma Joan always says, "Just say it to the mirror." Personally, I've always written in a journal. In times of anger, I have said and written some pretty mean things. I'm certainly glad I'm the only one that read them, or heard them spoken. We can never take our words away and they can have a lasting effect on not only your family's happiness, but on yours as well. Get it out, but don't give it out.

Your Sunny Side: What is another way that you can vent without hurting others?

_____

_____

2. **You don't always have to talk.** Carly told me: "When my family and I have major disagreements we sing our anger out. It lightens the mood. We made an agreement that if we are all getting irritable with each other, instead of screaming out words we sing them out! It lightens the mood and makes us reconnect with each other as a family instead of being angry with one another."

Your Sunny Side: How can you express your feelings without saying cruel things? Is this a challenge for you?

_____

_____

3. **Keep a calm voice.** Be the bigger person, no matter how tempted or provoked you feel to shout a few lines. Raising your voice will only rile up the other party—leaving both of you in a tizzy. You will be received as more mature and more in control when you maintain a firm but peaceful tone.

Your Sunny Side: Do you have trouble refraining from raising your voice? What can you do to rein yourself in?

_____

Anger, especially at high levels or for long periods of time, is not a healthy emotion. Both physically and mentally, it wears away at our concentration, our peace, and our happiness. If you've ever been really upset with someone, then you know how much energy it takes to maintain that kind of intense feeling for a prolonged period of time. Holding a grudge doesn't just punish the person you're mad at, it also punishes you. Let yourself be happy by letting go and moving on with your life, even if people, including family members, have hurt you. You don't have to forget or condone their behavior but it will do you good to forgive. Holding on to that pain, anger, and sadness will prevent you from obtaining the happiness you deserve. Give it up and get going with your life.

As we grow up, a great deal of our anger can surface because we learn about so many realities. Our parents may not be the perfect people we thought they were when we were children. Our best friend betrays us, or someone we love passes away suddenly. As children, we are often sheltered from the harsh realities of our world so that we may enjoy somewhat of a blissful ignorance in childhood. Finding out the truth as we age can be a painful realization. There goes gravity…taking our castles on clouds down from the sky.

If we are wise, we can learn to accept the truth and use our knowledge to help others and ourselves. We can learn from the mistakes of our parents and we can try to model what they did *right*. Part of love is accepting our family for who they are—warts and all. It doesn't mean that our family members have to be our best friends, but if we can come to a level of acceptance where we realize that they are not angels or demons, but simply people, just like us, then we will be in a good place.

But because parents are people, that means they aren't perfect. Yet many of us still feel an obligation to abide by our parent's wishes. Sometimes our mom's wish for us is that we will lose twenty pounds and she has to tell you this every day. Sometimes our dad's wish is for us to major in neuroscience when psychology just isn't good enough. These wishes aren't our wishes, though. You need to go where you'll fall in love with what **you** love to do—not what your parents will love. When you go for your own goals, your happiness will ensue because it's what you want, not because it's what your parents want.

Sunny Suggestion

Have a supportive mentor in mind. If you're living with your own wicked stepmother of sorts, who doesn't allow you to pursue your dreams, try to be polite while you simultaneously do your own thing. Next step: find a support system--and it doesn't have to come from the token two people you'd think of right off the bat (aka mom and dad). It doesn't even have to be a relative. According to a study by Sherman, Lansford, and Volling in 2006, you don't need a sibling to be successful in life (good news to me), but you do need a best friend. You just need someone who'll love you for being you.

Your Sunny Side: How supportive have your parents been of your dreams? Do you feel like they hold you back or help you?

_____

_____

If you have a passion, I hope your family can recognize that and support you in all the ways they can. If they're smart, they'll realize that you'll be much more successful doing what you love rather than what they would love. At the same time, try to be patient as you try to compromise with your family. They may still be working with dial-up while you're on high speed broadband. If they don't have faith in your goals and dreams, help them by proving not only to them, but to yourself that you are worthy of what you love to do.

I don't know how you feel about your family. It's hard to write about a topic as complex as family because some of you adore yours—every Christmas, every birthday, and every day is special because they are in your life. For others, your family may be a source of great pain, burden, and sadness. Perhaps you have endured physical, verbal, sexual, or emotional abuse and perhaps you feel like you have no escape. Let me be your Wilson Phillips here and tell you "to hold on for one more day." (Refer to the end of *Bridesmaids* if you just raised an eyebrow).

No matter how your family has contributed or detracted to your life, I hope you are confident in knowing that your happiness is still ensured. While you cannot choose your family, you can still choose happiness. We alone decide how we will look back on our childhood; we can have an appreciation for the lessons we were taught (both from the good and the bad examples) or we can resent our past. I don't recommend the latter. If you felt like you were put down a lot when you were younger, don't stay down. Get up! Fight harder. We don't always get a fair start in life and yes, some do have to work much harder to find their place, but you can still do what you dream. Let your family help fuel you to do great things.

And someday when it's time to have your own family, I hope you will live with this mindset: **"The man travels the world in search of what he needs, and returns home to find it."**

—George Moore, novelist

If your home was a safe haven as a child, recreate that for your own children someday so that they may grow from the same love that you received. But if your home life was fraught with hardship, build a better home than the one you had. Just because you had a challenging experience once in your life doesn't mean it needs to be recreated. Break the cycle and start new traditions. A home is where is a happy heart is—you can create that on your own with or without a house.

The Sunshine
of Success

Most of the time I hear people say they imagine their happiness to be a distant dream to one day enjoy. They're waiting for their magic potion (and no, it does not consist of Adderall contrary to some collegiate opinions) to help them graduate, they're hoping for their love-at-first-sight prince charming, and they're fantasizing of the home that they'll live happily ever after in (inspiration a la Pinterest). But why entrap yourself as a lifelong Little Mermaid? Some people are eighty years old and still wishing for their pair-of-legs moment when they'll finally have the chance to be truly happy. You can be happy now if you're willing to be humble and grateful. Happiness comes with loving what you have, not wishing for what you want.

The reality is that there's a trade-off to everything—remember how Ariel lost her voice and nearly the love of her life? (And hey, let's be honest, in the Hans Christian Anderson fairytale, she actually dies—not to be a downer or anything). But ultimately, because she's a magical princess, life turned out like Disney intended—she did get the prince, the castle, and she got her voice back. But sometimes, like Sebastian suggests, we have to settle in the sea. That's not necessarily a bad thing—we have to find our happiness no matter where we are in our lives, be it location or life circumstances. The grass, or in Ariel's case, land, is often not as green on the other side. The key to finding true happiness is to enjoy it while you're living your life, not while you're holding out for it.

As much as I love Disney, life is usually not a fairytale romance. It's real—sometimes we have to jump from apartment to apartment until the time we can afford that dream home. Unquestionably, marrying for love will bring you happiness but marrying for money won't. Don't wed a paycheck, wed the person who will enlighten your life. What's important is that we are always working in a positive direction so that we know we can build ourselves back up when we break down. You'll have so much more appreciation for what you *do* have in your life when you've earned it. Even a magic spell isn't that powerful—true happiness comes from within.

I like to think that life is perfect in its imperfection. Happiness can even come from the moments when we can be aware of the negatives in our lives, but still choose to emphasize a positive perspective. There's always something to sing about—you just need to give yourself the voice, like Ariel did. (Clearly *The Little Mermaid* is my favorite Disney movie.).

We have to remember what makes us happy in life and keep that in the forefront of our minds. We are at an age where we have many decisions to make—what to major in, what to apply for in terms of education and internships, and where to live—and with these decisions, we need to factor in our happiness. As easy as it can be to feel swayed by college rankings, prestigious companies, and moving far away to get a "real" college experience, we have to make our happiness a priority in our decisions. Because only with this mindset, rather than a mindset of making money or pleasing other people, can we start living a life of *our* success—not someone else's.

We all ultimately want success in our life. Whether it is to be a successful CEO or a successful homemaker, we all want to leave a positive legacy behind. We want people to remember us fondly when we're gone and love us while we're still here. And while success, in the financial sense, is a relevant predictor of your happiness, a successful life in *your* eyes is essential for your ultimate happiness. So what does success mean to you?

Sunny Samples

1. Kyle: "I used to think that success is about who had the biggest house and the nicest cars. That has changed a lot for me as I've realized having those things doesn't necessarily make you happy. Instead, I think success is defined by happiness. Success is unquestionably related to doing well and having a good paying job, but that doesn't matter at all if you're not happy."

2. Kara: "Getting good grades makes me happy for an instant. But if I were to base my idea of success solely on getting a 4.0, I wouldn't be a very happy person. There is no lasting joy in acing a test, however I believe there is lasting joy in helping other people."

3. Andrea: "I think success is defined by reaching the goals you set for yourself. Right now, I just graduated from a university with a degree and job. I feel successful because I am starting my career. I love my job, and that makes me so happy. I haven't reached the end goal in my career but working towards it makes me feel very happy."

4. Sean: "Success is becoming the best that you're capable of becoming. I don't think I'm successful, because I'm still 'under construction.' I have potential to be successful in regards to what I want out of my career, my family, and my life, but I haven't gotten there yet. This doesn't bother me, because I'm making the effort and moving in the right direction."

5. Kayla: "I think success needs to be defined by each individual—it is impossible to have a definition of success that fits every single person. Even within each person there are different kinds of success. For me, being surrounded by friends that I love is a success. Landing my amazing internship at Boeing is also a success—but in a very different way. I consider myself very successful by my own terms, but I will always have things that I'm working on in all aspects of my life."

Want to find success in your own life? It is essential that we pay attention to what our head and our heart are telling us. If you're being pulled in two directions by what you think you *should* do with your life and what you *actually* want to do, here are some Sunny Suggestions to help you take a step in the right direction.

Sunny Suggestions

1. Find mentors. I credit much of my success to the mentors who have guided me in my decisions. Ever since I read John Wooden's *A Game Plan for Life: The Power of Mentoring* I've been inspired to reach out to people who I think will make a difference in my life and indeed, they have. I highly encourage you to do the same. You meet certain people in your life for a reason—you can't just let them pass you by. Make the most of the mentors in your life, whether they give some advice over a matter of months or over a lifetime.

Your Sunny Side: Who are five people who have mentored you and how have they changed your life for the better? Or, if you haven't had any mentors yet, who would you like inspiration from?

1. _____

2. _____

3. _____

4. _____

5. _____

2. Explore your options. You may have a clear path or it may seem like the road is twisting and turning twenty different ways. It's so important to explore all of your career interests so you don't have that midlife "what if" moment. Even if you think your ideal career is far-fetched, like being an animator for Pixar or a pediatric cardiologist, get as close as you can to the action so you can make the best decision possible. You'll have to work extra hard, but it's worth it to get an insider perspective. Get the best internships you can find, take classes that are in alignment with what you'd like to potentially do, and again, find mentors who help you make it happen.

Your Sunny Side: What are five different careers that interest you and what steps can you take to get some hands-on experience in each?

1. _____

2. _____

3. _____

4. _____

5. _____

3. Look back on your life. Think of what you enjoyed studying, what extracurricular activities you loved, what you did with your free time when you were a child—what is it that you were drawn to? If you're looking for guidance in your future, chances are, your past may give you the best hint. My hairstylist, Summer, always said that the hair color you had as a kid looks best when you're an adult—the same is often true when it comes to our careers. Incorporating what we loved as children can be a great indicator of what will bring us success and happiness as adults.

Your Sunny Side: What are five things you loved to do as a kid and how do you think each one could influence your career path?

1. _____

2. _____

3. _____

4. _____

5. _____

Setting Your Sights on Success

Personally, I like to recognize success in my life every day. Sure, we need something to look forward to but we should also strive to recognize our accomplishments in the here and now. I'm sure you've heard it said that we are often our biggest critic. But if we know we've done our absolute best for the day, I think that deserves a personal pat on the back. It's important that we take the time to praise our efforts rather than constantly put ourselves down for not meeting a personal expectation.

I'm not telling you to be narcissistic. In fact, that is one of the worst forms of happiness—it is an absolute cop-out and you're only deluding yourself if your life revolves solely for your personal happiness. Instead, my point is that you need to love yourself rather than feel like you've let yourself down. You don't always have to like what you do, but you should always strive to love who you are. A successful day is one where you can be proud of yourself and know that you did the right thing. You helped the person who dropped their books, you turned in an A-worthy essay, you treated your friend just because—you did things that made you a well-educated, compassionate person. You told someone you love them, you forgave someone or asked for forgiveness, you read a good book. If you're making a positive contribution, at least for the day, I think that sanctifies the term "success." If you have enough days like these, it becomes a lifetime of happiness.

Success is not necessarily one overarching achievement that defines your life. Sure, it may feel like the pinnacle at certain points, but that is only part of it. Success comes in small steps. Rewarding yourself along the way, rather than just when you reach the summit, makes all the difference. You will feel so much happier with yourself when you can recognize your hard work and treat yourself for it. Let yourself be happy if you've worked hard—you deserve it.

You have to enjoy the view along the way because you never know when your path may change. One thing I've noticed from my internships is that people are always coming and going. It's rare to see someone stay with a company for 30 years anymore. People move, marriages are made, babies are born and life is a constant ebb and flow. If you think your happiness will only come along with your executive title, Lamborghini, and mansion in Malibu, you're going to be waiting awhile. Maybe forever. I'm not saying you can't do it, because I believe you can if you're willing to work hard enough, but is that really where your happiness should come from? It's something to think about. I've thought about it and my answer is a resounding "no."

Success is comprised of so many components, but success in this day and age is often classified in terms of our careers. In our sometimes-warped thinking we may believe happiness is brought about by money, power and titles. This couldn't be further from the truth. When you build your joy on the sands of societal success, you're bound to sink at some point. Sure, there is reason to celebrate when you get hired, land a promotion or pull off a big event at work. But this is temporary. Fleeting. If you want to live a truly successful life, you've got to invest in more than just your bank account. You've got to invest in your relationships—you've got to love the people who will love you no matter how much money you make. Genuine bonds create genuine happiness—the bank can't ever take that away.

We have some big decisions on the horizon. As we prepare to enter the work world, we have to ask ourselves some serious questions. How much balance do we want in our life? Do we want our professional life to be the pound and our family to be the feather in our life? Or do we want it vice versa? A bit of both? This is a question that both men and women are asking themselves and it's never been more relevant during this era where women and men are working equally hard in the workforce.

This is why I'm such a big advocate for internships. There's no way you can really know what you want to do with your life until you've had the opportunity to see what your dream job really looks like in the daylight. Sometimes the airbrushed catalog of a career can look much more appealing than it actually is. What you see on TV or movies is often a façade; watching Grey's Anatomy to inspire your desire to be a doctor, or seeing The Today Show every morning in hopes of becoming an anchor, may not serve you well because it can glamorize the reality of the situation. It may help in your research, but you've got to get a behind-the-scenes bird's eye view on your potential career so that you can see what *really* happens at work.

I got to see everything when I interned for NBC Network News. I had a fantastic experience there watching Brian Williams do the national broadcast of *Nightly News* live in studio and chatting in the stairs with Bill Nye the Science Guy (we 90's kids would appreciate that one). Every day was different—I never knew who I would meet, what stories we would cover, or, what car Jay Leno would drive on the lot. But there was one blatant problem that I couldn't ignore—many of these people didn't have families. Or if they did, their nanny was on call 24/7.

I struggled with this all summer as I debated what I wanted to do with my life. What is it that truly matters to me? Having a successful career or being a successful mom? In a field like the news, it's hard to have both when you have to be ready to cover a story any second. And these are not just choices that I need to consider as a twenty-something—but as someone who, someday may be a wife and mother. It's a tough choice, especially if, like myself, you're driven to be an independent working woman. I still haven't ultimately decided what I want to do with my career, but seeing the facts instead of just hearing the stories gave me a whole new perspective. These decisions are never easy but keeping our happiness in mind is a great start. Here's what some of you had to say about your work experiences.

Sunny Samples

1. Kelsey: "I've worked at a florist shop, a surf shop, been a nanny, and interned at the Offices of the District Attorney and Public Defender. Having a job tends to make me happy because I feel like I am doing something productive and I highly value productivity. I think, in most jobs, there are so many lessons to be learned and positive experiences to be gained. As well as this, I have been able to increase my happiness by bringing a positive and willing attitude to work. Living in the moment, appreciating the ability to do something meaningful, and working with great people has the potential to be powerfully positive."

2. Julianne: "When I was in town for the summer and I first found out that I got hired at the new yogurt shop, I was ecstatic! This may seem odd especially considering the amazing internships my friends were getting, however this was a big deal for me. Since I was an athlete in high school and always had at least two sports to train for, I was never able to get a summer job. As a result, my resume, at best, was lacking. But when I got this job at the new shop, I was thrilled. This excitement was before I found out how amazingly kind my new bosses are and how entertaining my coworkers are. It's a simple job. We come in, clean, serve everyone with a smile, and try to create a happy experience for everyone who walks in the door. But coming into work, unlike other jobs, puts me into a great mood every time. I haven't had one shift where I don't laugh or smile. Yes, I work at a yogurt shop while my friends are interning for design companies and news stations, but right now, I could not be happier where I am. Sometimes in life, the simple things are what can make you the happiest."

3. Melissa: "I am an autistic aid to an 11 year old boy who I adore. I absolutely love my job. I feel like I am making a real difference in his life when I work with him. When I am with him we work on social skills as well as life skills. The smile on his face when he does a good job makes my day and he has definitely affected my happiness."

4. Josh: "I've had a lot of work-study jobs during the school year. Those weren't that fun, because I was doing it solely for money to afford school. Because there wasn't much of a figurative payout in building my future plans, I would have preferred to spend my time doing other things—like studying. On the other hand, most of my internships weren't that bad. Despite the fact that I did most of them for free, I knew that these were all stepping stones, so regardless of whether the work was engaging or not, I thought it was worth my time. I was happy knowing that I was walking toward the direction I wanted to go."

5. Rebecca: "I am in my first real job right now as a reporter for a local T.V. news station. I love what I do. I am so passionate about journalism because I am passionate about people. Every day I do something different. Every day is an adventure and every day I get to meet new people. I help people tell their stories and it's so rewarding. I am pursuing and living my passion."

What and where we choose to work can make or break us. It's one of the crucial decisions of our lives, especially in these early years. Of course, you can always change your path, but the longer you walk down your road, the harder and longer it takes to turn back and find a new trail. Sometimes we don't have the option of choosing where we want to work, but I hope you'll try and find the best possible fit for you based on your interests and your passions. Be patient with yourself in your pursuit and don't ever give up your dreams. You can never expect automatic success, but you can most definitely earn it if you're willing to work hard.

Sunny Suggestions

1. Define it. Success is hard to find if you don't know what you're looking for. We all have our own definitions of success but for me, it starts with happiness. Whenever I get that feeling of overjoy when I can't help but smile and (yes, for me, it includes a little dance) then I know it's been a true success. Whether it's getting a phone call that I got the job or going on a great date, it's something to celebrate. If you're happy and you know it—then let yourself be happy! (And clap your hands!)

Your Sunny Side: What does success mean to you?

_____

_____

2. Recognize it. Give yourself the credit you deserve. Don't dismiss your hard work. This isn't being cocky, it's being confident in your skill set and your potential. Build your self-esteem by building up your happiness. Being humble is very important but don't discredit yourself either. Especially if you're a girl, own up to your success! As women we are often taught to underestimate ourselves or belittle our accomplishments, but those days are gone. If you want to be successful, whether it's in the workplace, as a student or as an athlete, you need to be confident in your abilities and talents. You have a good hint of what you are capable of if you remind yourself what you've achieved.

Your Sunny Side: What are five successes you've had in your life?

1. _____

2. _____

3. _____

4. _____

5. _____

When you succeed at something, how does it affect your happiness?

_____

_____

3. Celebrate it. You don't need to shove your successes in everyone's face but you should celebrate your accomplishments with the people you love. Go out to a new restaurant, get an ice cream sundae, buy a new book—whatever you like—to reward yourself when you've worked hard. If you don't ever capitalize on what you've earned, then you won't be as motivated to keep reaching higher goals. We loved getting gold stars as kids—give them to yourself now in other ways when you've earned it.

Your Sunny Side: What are three ways you can celebrate a success?

1. _____

2. _____

3. _____

Having Your Manolo Moment

Much of the time—well let me correct myself—nearly all of the time, we work because we want, and need, money. You've heard the common adage: "Money can't buy happiness." But quite frankly, I think money *can* buy happiness if we earned it honestly and spend it wisely. You're even more golden if you're actually happy while you make money, working someplace that you love.

There are other ways that money *buffers* your happiness. Multiple studies have shown that living in a poor-socioeconomic environment can greatly affect your happiness. In fact, low-income individuals are far more likely to have significant health problems (Gallo & Matthews, 2003) and higher rates of psychopathology, criminal behavior, and substance abuse (Costello, Compton, Keeler, & Angold 2003, Cutrona et al., 2005). All of which I think we can safely say, are not the definition of happiness. So while having money won't guarantee your happiness, it can help guard against some of the threats poverty may bring to you. Nevertheless, I wanted to put the money maxim to the test. Here's your two cents.

Sunny Samples

1. Peter: "I know they say money doesn't bring happiness, as there are plenty of wealthy people that have their own lion's share of issues. It isn't money itself that brings me happiness, but the peace of mind and security that comes with it. Money is a tool to enhance my life, not to define it."

2. Wendy: "Paychecks, like your GPA, are a quantitative way to describe how you are doing in your career, so it's easy to forget what's important in life and base your self-worth on a number. I've been guilty of that before, but I'm definitely working on it."

3. Jessica: "I think that money can and should only affect happiness to an extent. Having a certain amount of money allows us to reach a certain level of security. Not having to stress about making ends meets is a weight off our shoulders and therefore allows us to live a happier and more carefree life. However, the danger comes when people make money the focus of their life. When you see wealth in that way, I don't think it's possible to be happy because there will always be someone richer or with a fancier car."

I couldn't agree more. We certainly need money to survive, but it can quickly represent the bane of our existence if we live for making money rather than modestly enjoying what our money can bring. Just like alcohol or gambling, money, or the symbol of it, can become an addiction. And no addiction, even if it's for something like love, can, for that matter, ever make us truly happy or healthy. Life should be lived in moderation if we want to experience a natural happiness. While that price tag varies for everyone, idolizing money as the sole source of your happiness is a slippery slope. Remember that golden word: *balance*.

Sunny Suggestions

1. Be at peace. Maybe making and spending money is no big deal for you and maybe it is one of the biggest stressors in your life right now. The key is to get organized about your money and know how much you can appropriately spend. Don't trick yourself into thinking you have a number that you don't—no one wants to be the person who can't pay for their dinner. You'll be much happier if you can be honest with yourself and realize where you are rather than imagining you're already where you want to be.

Your Sunny Side: How does money affect your happiness?

_____

_____

Are you content with how much money you have now or do you feel like you'll only be happy once you have a certain amount. Why?

_____

_____

2.   Be smart about saving. There's no magic pill that will make you wake up one day in the 1200 thread count, Egyptian cotton bed sheets you've been eying at Pottery Barn. Simply put: you've got to be smart about your money today if you want to be successful tomorrow.

Your Sunny Side: What are three ways you can be smarter about saving your money?

1. _____

2. _____

3. _____

3.   Save, Budget, Spend Wisely. I always save 25% of every paycheck in my savings account. You never know what might happen (ideally a surprise vacation to Italy?) so it's best if you can store some of your earnings away on a regular basis—at least 10%. It's also important to save some of your money for donations to various charities you connect with. Once you've done this, you can budget your money by designating how much maximum spending you can do per month on food, clothing, etc. I highly recommend getting an app to make the work easier for you—I use Mint on my phone on a regular basis and it helps me keep in check. Lastly, when you do need to spend money, ask yourself the old adage—"do I really need this?" Pay attention to the shopping you do (and how often you do it), and whether your purchases are truly price efficient. Don't deprive yourself but don't delude yourself either—you'll be much happier if you're spending is within reason.

Your Sunny Side: How much would you like to save out of your paycheck? _____

What can you do to hold yourself accountable to a budget?

_____

_____

When you're going to buy something, what can you do to make sure you are spending smart?

_____

Growing Out of the Peter Pan Mentality

Success is a word that we are constantly hearing—no pressure, right? We're all getting asked on a regular basis, "so what do you want to do with your future?" Pardon me for not having a two-page answer. Instead, how about this answer? In my future, I would like to be happy. How's that for a start? There may be no telling what career we'll end up with in twenty years, what our kids will be like, or where we'll settle down. But thankfully we will always have a compass and it's guided by our happiness. If we are willing to follow that internal navigator instead of maps that are marked by societal pressures, then we'll end up exactly where we're meant to be.

More than anything, when I think of the future for myself, I want to have the people that I love in my life on a daily basis. I want to cook Christmas dinner with my mom, and when the day comes, I want to dance with my dad at my wedding. I want to have the moment when "you just know" that you are meant to be with that certain, special person for the rest of your life. I want to have a healthy child (yes, okay, preferably a girl but yes, I know everything happens for a reason—I just love pink so darn much!) I want to have my own little Siamese cat who is almost as loyal to me as a yellow lab (you dog lovers, you...). I want to be a successful writer that brings happiness to my readers, motivating them to live their happiest lives, in the way that I am striving to find my own. I want to meet the people of this world who have made a profound difference in the lives of others, and someday, I hope that I can be among them.

Also, I want to have health, so I'll never have to hear the words, "You have cancer," or any other disease. I want to laugh every day and I want to show someone love whenever I get the chance. I never want to yell, I never want to cause someone emotional or physical pain, and I never want to consciously make the wrong decision. I know I won't end every day feeling happy, but I do want to end every day feeling happily hopeful for the next. I always want to have the hunger for happiness in my life (and for a good meal.). That is unlikely to ever to go away. Here's what some of you hope for in your futures.

Sunny Samples

1. Grace: "When I think of my future and what will make me happy, I envision being married and having endless adventures, while maintaining a stable career. I like to think about all those times ahead of me, including starting my own family (which will include a golden retriever, of course). I am excited for those fantastic milestones in life, as well as the tiny little things that make me happy on a daily basis—like in the morning when I'm listening to NPR on the way to work. I look forward to all these things, and remember to appreciate them now since I'm already living my dream!"

2. Kurt: "What would make me most happy is to secure a job where I wake up every morning happy to go to work. I've been through enough things in my life that I haven't enjoyed doing. The most important thing is doing something that I love. I also know that I want to eventually find that person that I will be with for the rest of my life."

3. Cassidy: "I used to think this answer was so straight forward. I would be happy in my future if I had my career in line and worked at least 50 hours a week being a big time event planner. Just recently however, my answer has blurred. I used to imagine my life as coming home to a nice apartment and my dogs, at the end of the day. But now I'm thinking more about the people who would be there when I come home. I think I would be happy to be in a long term committed relationship, with someone I love who makes me happy, as well as their having an extremely successful and rewarding career. Someone who makes me laugh and meshes well with my family, as I hope to with his."

4.   Annie: "When I think of my future, having a healthy, loving family would make me the happiest. I believe that family is the thing that matters most in this life. And I also believe that experiencing life with people you love, respect, and have fun with only adds joy to every experience."

5.   Kelly: "In my opinion happiness is not something you can pin point. Each day I define happiness differently. So in regards to my future happiness, I do not know exactly what will make me happy, but I am excited to find out."

It's true; we never know exactly where life will take us. We can guide our lives and set our sails, but ultimately the wind can blow certain people and certain things into our lives that we never expected. It's our job as the captains to take on both the hard-hitting waves and the gentle breezes as they come by. And better yet, that we soak up the sun when it shines on our vessel. I hope you sail into your own success every day.

Sunny Suggestion

Dream away. You never know what may happen in your life—all the more reason to dream. As important as it is to be in the present, a lot of our happiness can come from hoping for an even happier future. Everyone has different hopes for the coming years; knowing yours will help you have a better understanding for who you are. When you know what you're looking for, it will be that much easier to find it.

Your Sunny Side: What do you see for your future happiness?

_____

_____

_____

So, as we say farewell for now, I leave you with this final quote by one of my favorite poets, Ralph Waldo Emerson:

"To laugh often and much; to win the respect of intelligent people and the affection of children…to leave the world a better place…to know even one life has breathed easier because you lived. This is to have succeeded."

Only a few can become extremely successful in monetary success but we can all be successful if we live by Emerson's belief. Small acts can lead to enormous successes if we are devoted to making not only our lives, but also the lives of others, all together wonderful and delightfully happy. We all can have that. Happiness is yours for the taking.

Conclusion

ell, we've come to the end of this yellow brick road. I think it's been a golden-good-time—I hope it has been so for you as well. My goal is that you not only leave these pages feeling a little, or even better, A LOT happier, but also that you know what it is that makes you happy.

I hope that you can start to see the world in a different way. I hope that you start to notice that simple joys of this life and I also hope that you'll recognize the profound blessings you have. These gifts may come in small packages and they may be in disguise but, nonetheless, they are blessings. Life is too short to be preoccupied with the petty—instead preoccupy with the precious. I am convinced that you have gifts in your life that have been given to you, just as I am equally assured that you have so many gifts to give. Be grateful for what you have been given, and be generous with what you give.

One concern I've had while writing this is that I don't want you to leave with the impression that seeking your own happiness is selfish. Happiness should be shared. Yes, it is a pursuit brought about by self-interest but it helps the interest of others when it is done right. Happiness is more than just a personal conquest. It's about a team mission. It's like the difference between lust and love. Lust is all about instant gratification, pleasure, even consumption if you will—gluttony for the infatuated. But love is pure and true, like genuine happiness. When you seek it for the right reasons, you will be rewarded with the right answers. When we make others happy, our happiness increases as a natural by-product.

As I leave you (just for now!) I think it's only fitting that I impart the essentials I've learned from this research.

Sunny Suggestions

1. **Write down your Five Daily Gratitudes**: Any time of day—look around and see what it is that you have to be thankful for. Even on the worst day, I can guarantee that there is not only one, but at least five things in your life that you can be thankful for. This will be a life changer for you.

2. **Strive to achieve something on your Sunny Set**: Right this instant, you might not be able to get on a plane and head over to Italy to achieve your goal of eating gelato in front of Trevi Fountain, but you can start working toward it. Make plans for your life—no one but you can make them. Furthermore, hold yourself accountable and check back on your list from time to time. Your goals will go gray if you don't get gutsy with your life.

3. **Interact with a friend**: If you can be with them, then head on over to your pal's place. But if you can't, then make use of the technology we have and chat on Skype or use some other source. Don't go a day without saying hello to at least one person that you care about. Communication is key. Humans are inherently social creatures and isolating ourselves is the quickest way to lose your happiness. Don't put yourself in a personal prison—interact with your friends as much as you can. Chat, text, call, comment, and use any and all means to do so as much as you can!

4. **Do something for yourself**: As much as I said you need to be social, you also need some time to find serenity for yourself. When you take the time to keep your spirits high, you'll be able to lift up others even higher. You deserve to take some time to just be with yourself. Because if you don't relax, you won't be ready to rumble! Balance is key.

5. **Find a challenge**: We are happier when we are setting goals for ourselves. Even if we don't fully achieve them, we feel so much more content with ourselves when we've at least given those goals a go. So make yourself proud and pursue what it is you are yearning for. It's much better to wish for a better future than to look back and wish you did better.

6. Spend time with your family or a mentor—or both! I find that we are so much more productive and happy when we are inspired. When we are surrounding ourselves with the people who inspire us the most—our parents, our coaches, or our teachers for example—we are motivated to be better. Life is a losing game if we aren't constantly learning, and it's our job to make sure we ask questions and heed the advice of the people who inspire us on a daily basis.

7. Look back on your happy memories: Sometimes when going through a challenging time we get tunnel vision. We can't remember our former happy days or imagine a better future to come. But it's especially important when you feel like you're in a rut to keep your fond times in your forefront. Remind yourself of the people who have added a tremendous amount of joy to your life—look back on pictures, old birthday cards, and home videos to remember some of your best memories. Also, I highly recommend keeping a positive journal of all your greatest adventures, successes, and happy experiences. Once it's on the page, you can remember it forever by reading it over again and again.

8. Laugh: I can't stress this one enough! It's happiness in its most natural state. Do what you can to laugh every day—get laughter from people, TV shows, or websites. Even a good tickle can do the trick!

9. Make things right: Whether you've been wronged or you've wronged against others, set things straight. The longer you withhold forgiveness or delay asking for it, the more miserable you'll be. You won't get that genuine happiness until you feel at peace with the people in your life. Let go of your pride and give the apologies that others deserve. Let go of the pain you've held on to and find it in your heart to forgive. You'll feel so much better once you do both.

10. Volunteer: As young adults it's easy to make life all about ourselves—our problems become our universe. But when we take the time to look outside of our own (extremely little) world, we'll see that when viewing and taking in the full scope of the world there are vastly bigger problems. We all should lend a hand. Knowing that you've made a contribution, be it in time, money, or brain power, you can go to sleep a little happier knowing that you didn't stand idly by, you ran to the aid of others. Volunteer throughout your life and your happiness will grow alongside your giving.

As I prepare to bid adieu, I want to reiterate how much I've enjoyed this entire process of researching, writing, and editing. I feel so fortunate to have had the opportunity to see beyond the confines of my own world—and to have the chance to look into yours. Thank you for opening the window that let me see so much more than my own view. I am so incredibly grateful to each and every one of you who shared your thoughts on happiness with me.

As I say farewell for now, I hope you'll go out, in full force, with your own ideas and wishes, rather than wait for your life to happen. **Happiness happens when you make it happen**. I wish you all the best and I thank you for letting me share this journey with you. We are so much stronger when we collaborate as a team rather than confiscate ourselves to be a lone individual. We need each other just to get through, let alone to be happy.

May you find happiness wherever you go. I think you'll find that the happiness you discover has been within you all along. You just have to hunker down when it's missing and hold on to it when you have it. Happiness is never out of reach, sight, or mind. Happiness is here, now, present, and always will be. May you take pride in your life, realize the power of the your dreams, and celebrate happiness today and every day.

Keep shining,

The Sunny Girl, Lauren Cook

The Sunny Girl's Sunny Set

1. **Sing in the high school talent show.** I sang "I Will Always Love You" and actually won third place.
2. Hatch and raise a chick.
3. Study abroad in Italy.
4. **Go to UCLA.** I'm so excited to say that I'm a proud Bruin!
5. **Work for Disney.** I was so honored to work for Disney ABC Television Group in their photo department. I will always be grateful to have that experience.
6. Marry the husband of my dreams.
7. Have a daughter.
8. Go to every place in *1,000 Places to See Before You Die.*
9. Go skydiving.
10. Go hang-gliding.
11. Get my SCUBA degree.
12. **See the cast of Twilight.** My roommate and I went to the *New Moon* premiere in Westwood and we saw the entire cast.
13. Meet Julie Andrews.
14. Get baptized.
15. Get an agent.
16. Star in a Broadway musical.
17. Have a star in Hollywood.

18. Be a Disney Princess at Disneyland.
19. Get Bachelor's degrees in Psychology and Communications.
20. Get a Master's degree.
21. Get certified in counseling.
22. Live in a beautiful, sunny, and personally decorated home.
23. Own a Siamese cat.
24. Compete in a ballroom dance competition.
25. Meet Miss America.
26. Earn one million dollars by age twenty-five.
27. Be a New York Times bestselling author.
28. Go on the Ellen DeGeneres show.
29. Meet Oprah.
30. Own a pair of Manolos!
31. Be a paid professional motivational speaker.
32. Volunteer over 5,000 hours of community service.
33. Build a house with Habitat for Humanity.
34. **Plant, grow, and eat from my own garden.** I had tomatoes, peppers, and carrots. But the best was the zucchini- I made the most delicious bread with it!
35. Get tested for BRCA I/II genes.
36. Meet the President.
37. **See the Capitol and White House.** I had an amazing time with my mom visiting Washington D.C. The cherry blossoms made it all the more beautiful.
38. Watch a Supreme Court session. Well, I've been inside the court but seating is very limited so I'll have to try again next time.
39. Go on an African safari.
40. Swim with a whale.
41. Go diving in the coral reef.
42. Swim with sharks.
43. Eat gelato in Italy.
44. Learn to speak Italian.
45. Ski Cornis in Mammoth.
46. Make wine by stomping grapes.

47. Have a beautiful, classy, and pink wedding!
48. **Join a sorority.** I am a proud Chi Omega sister for life!
49. Watch all the top AFI 100 movies. Getting there! I'm about halfway through.
50. Go to the Olympics.
51. Show a pig in the fair.
52. Sew a cross stitch picture and frame it.
53. Raise one-hundred-thousand dollars for the American Cancer Society. I'm at about seventy-thousand for now.
54. Go to a sumo-wrestling event.
55. Swim with dolphins in the wild.
56. Play with children in Africa.
57. Walk on the Great Wall of China.
58. Speak fluent Spanish.
59. Tour the rainforest and hold a monkey.
60. Have my own talk show.
61. Record a CD.
62. Climb Mount Whitney.
63. **Read Harry Potter Series.** I think J.K. Rowling is one of the greatest authors of our time. Her mind amazes me.
64. Hike Half Dome.
65. Pet and hold a tiger.
66. Pet and hold a lion.
67. See the pyramids.
68. **Go to the Smithsonian.** Lincoln's hat and Dorothy's red slippers were my favorites. I could spend a month in these museums!
69. Go to an Eagle's concert.
70. Two-step in Texas.
71. Ride a donkey through the Grand Canyon.
72. **Make delicious crème brulee!** My best friend Lauren and I had the best time making my favorite custard; especially once we realized that the recipe called for egg yolks, NOT egg whites. Oops.
73. Go skinny-dipping in the ocean.
74. Watch a space shuttle launch.

75. Fly first class.

76. Ride a camel.

77. Sit on a jury.

78. Visit Walden Pond and read Thoreau there.

79. **Go dancing at a Hollywood club.** Just like "Night at the Roxbury!"

80. Go to Oktoberfest in Germany.

81. **Visit Winchester Mansion.**

82. Spend the night in a haunted house.

83. See a ghost.

84. Get passionately kissed in New York Times Square on New Year's.

85. Get beads during Mardi Gras.

86. Tour America—road trip style.

87. Sing karaoke in front of everyone.

88. Go ride in a hot air balloon.

89. Learn to golf.

90. Gamble at a slot machine in Vegas.

91. Visit the Holy Land.

92. Visit Auschwitz concentration camp.

93. Run in a marathon.

94. **Fly a kite on the beach.** *Who cares if I was an 18 year old with a Barbie kite?*

95. Watch a movie at a drive in movie theater.

96. **Ride on the back of a motorcycle.** Nothing like riding down the Pacific Coast Highway listening to "Love Shack."

97. Ride a mechanical bull.

98. **Fire a gun.** My dad took me to the shooting range and I even hit the bull's eye! I loved getting to hold the pink revolver, too!

99. Go on a missionary trip.

100. Befriend a homeless person.

101. See the Northern Lights.

102. Break a world record.

103. Go on a police drive.

104. Run and kiss in the rain.

105. Write and publish a children's book.

106. **Write and publish a self-help book.** That's about to happen!
107. Take cooking lessons.
108. Go sailing.
109. Go cave diving where there will be human skulls!
110. Go on an archeology dig.
111. Get elected to a public office.
112. **Read the "Success Principles."** One of my favorite books of all time- Jack Canfield is one of my mentors.
113. Ride a gondola in Italy.
114. Witness a solar eclipse.
115. See SNL. Live.
116. Be the host of SNL.
117. Get a bowling score over 100. Still working on that…do bumpers count?
118. Write and publish a book of poetry.
119. Meet Tom Hanks.
120. **See the Magna Carta and the Constitution.** There you were Ben Franklin!
121. Go white-water rafting.
122. Go rock climbing.
123. Visit all 50 states.
124. **Get my fortune read.** He predicted my future as a speaker and he even said he saw a lot of "sunshine". He also sensed my immense amount of gratitude- I was amazed by how well he seemed to know me!
125. Sculpt a vase.
126. Visit Playboy mansion. Only for journalistic purposes of course.
127. **Knit an entire scarf.** I did it in three days with the help of my Grandma Joan. I made it for my mentor, Dallas Woodburn.
128. Grow a garden of beautiful flowers.
129. Donate a million dollars to the American Cancer Society.
130. Donate blood.
131. Spend the night at Hearst Castle.
132. Invent something and get a patent for it.

133. Start my own business.
134. Start my own restaurant.
135. Milk a cow.
136. Mush a dog sled team.
137. Watch turtles hatch on the beach.
138. See gorillas in the wild.
139. Feed a penguin.
140. Feed a sea otter.
141. Go to New York fashion week.
142. Visit the Titanic.
143. Travel to the moon.
144. See the Pope.
145. Complete my stamp collection.
146. See the Rockettes perform live.
147. Watch the Macy's Thanksgiving Day Parade live.
148. Be in the Macy's Thanksgiving Day Parade!
149. Plant a tree.
150. Read the entire Bible.
151. Dissect a human cadaver.
152. Watch a surgery performed.
153. Be on Dancing with the Stars.
154. Save a life.
155. See Elton John in concert.
156. See the American Ballet Academy perform Swan Lake and Romeo and Juliet.
157. Give a famous speech and be quoted for it.
158. Visit Antarctica.
159. Go to a blues bar in Chicago and eat at Gino's pizza.
160. Spend Saint Patrick's Day in Ireland.
161. Bathe in the Ganges River.
162. Participate in a tea ceremony in Japan.
163. Go to an Indian wedding.
164. Be in a music video.
165. Fly in a fighter jet.

166. Ride a horse on the beach.
167. Go polar bear watching.
168. Take a cruise along the Nile River.
169. Go to the Hershey's Chocolate factory and eat the whole chocolate bar right there.
170. Touch an orca.
171. **Get in UCLA Honor's Program.** I am in Alpha Lambda Delta and Phi Eta Sigma.
172. Hold a bald eagle.
173. Go to a real luau.
174. Own a pet rabbit.
175. Own a baby water turtle named Pebble.
176. Eat frogs' legs.
177. See a presidential inauguration.
178. Visit the United Nations.
179. **Pass all of my AP tests.** I even got a four on my AP Calculus Test! I was absolutely shocked- definitely the best surprise of my senior summer.
180. *Graduate at the top of my high school class.* Not Valedictorian or Salutatorian but that's okay- 4th place is just fine!
181. Cook with Paula Dean. There will be butter.
182. Play with a monkey.
183. Feed the homeless on Thanksgiving at a shelter.
184. **Get CPR license.**
185. Have a famous blog. I'm getting there I hope!
186. **Win Girl of the Year.** I was so honored to receive this award. There were so many amazing seniors in my class. As Captain said, we "Finish Strong!"
187. Attend a movie premiere.
188. Go to all the national parks.
189. Kiss on top of the Eiffel Tower.
190. Have a Jacuzzi bathtub.
191. Be an NCL Patroness.
192. Sit on the floor of a Laker's game.

193. Throw the first pitch at a baseball game.
194. Own a vacation beach home.
195. Be in a magic show at the Magic Castle.
196. Give a speech to over a million people.
197. Be the chair of a Relay for Life event.
198. **Vote in an election.** I have always been grateful for the privilege of voting. I registered on my 18th birthday and I was so excited to mark that ballot.
199. **Have an article published for a magazine.** My work was featured in Chi Omega's Eleusis magazine. I hope I'll have more opportunities to write for magazines!
200. Work for a magazine.
201. Meet Jack Canfield and work with him.
202. Watch Kentucky Derby.
203. Climb Mount Kilimanjaro.
204. Be on TIME's 100 most influential people list.
205. Hold a national conference where I am the keynote speaker.
206. **Join Toastmasters.**
207. Walk on the boardwalk at 2 A.M.
208. Pan for gold.
209. Fly with Blue Jets.
210. Watch a sunrise and sunset in the same day.
211. Take tour of Disney's underground system.
212. Have credits on IMDB.
213. Go on a Geocache adventure.
214. Raise a seeing-eye dog.
215. Be a model in a fashion show.
216. Walk in a peaceful protest.
217. Get name on Wikipedia.
218. **Take acting lessons with Acting Corps.** I have always loved acting and it was wonderful to learn more about the craft; I guess I loved it enough to drive three hours every day for a month.
219. Spend a night at the Madonna Inn.
220. Watch World Cup finals live.

221. **Be hypnotized.** I went for my phobia of vomit. That's right. And apparently I have three angels: Cherub, Lauren, and Mama. Really, now?
222. Graduate from college with honors.
223. Go zip lining.
224. Go to all the "1,000 Places to See Before I Die in America and Canada."
225. Go to the Sandals beach resort and "have the time of my life!"
226. Bike across California.
227. Perform in "Mamma Mia." I just want to wear the sequin body suit.
228. Go backpacking.
229. Walk in a breast cancer walk.
230. Speak at a woman's Christian conference.
231. Dive through a sunken ship.
232. Design and make a dress.
233. Hear Joel Osteen give a sermon live.
234. Join National Speaker's Association.
235. **Read the Happiness Project and write to Gretchen Rubin.** This book largely inspired this blog and my current goals. I wanted to write a Teen Edition with her but sadly, she rejected my offer. Yet I believe everything happens for a reason and here we are now—I published my own book!
236. Go ice blocking at UCLA.
237. Go tunneling at UCLA.
238. Attend the Academy Awards.
239. *Win Panhellenic New Member of the Year.* I did not win this but I was honored to be one of the top three candidates out of the Pledge Class of 2009- good enough for me!
240. Win Panhellenic Woman of the Year.
241. Dance 26 hours in Dance Marathon.
242. Go to Medieval Times!
243. Go on a Murder Mystery train ride.
244. Make sushi.
245. Sell over a million copies of my book.

246. Earn my Competent Communicator Award in Toastmasters.
247. Be on the Today Show.
248. Be on Good Morning America.
249. Have a Sunny Side Up room filled with everything yellow!
250. Learn how to BBQ.
251. Take a painting class.
252. Run in the Disney World Half Marathon.
253. Sew a patchwork quilt.
254. **Dance at a salsa club.** That Latin lover boy sure knew how to swing me around the floor!
255. **Grant a wish for a child with the Make-A-Wish Foundation.** We granted a wish for a sweet, five-year-old boy named Jayden. He wanted a dinosaur playground so we gave it to him.
256. Tour Europe with my girlfriends.
257. Have a monthly column in a national newspaper.
258. Have a best-selling book series.
259. Visit with Meryl Streep.
260. Have a dog to take walks with.
261. **Be happy.**

My Sunny
Sincerities

I'm in awe of the hundreds of people, especially teens and young adults, who have played an integral role in this process. From answering Facebook messages to elaborating in full-on interviews, I could never have written this book without the many people who were so generous with their time, and more importantly, with their hearts and minds. I am so thankful to everyone who answered even one of my questions—your commentary has always been insightful, inspirational, and intelligent. Thank you for trusting me enough to tell me your thoughts and thank you for caring enough to share them with everyone else.

Of all the interviewees, I especially want to thank the Woodburn family. Greg was wonderful enough to go through an in-depth interview regarding his organization, 'Give Running,' and Dallas has been my mentor before I even wrote a single word on the utterly white pages of my computer screen. Dallas, thank you for believing in me and thank you for setting such a shining example. I admire you more than you know.

I also want to express my sincere appreciation to my teachers who not only taught me how to write, but more importantly, taught me to believe in myself. Mr. Geib, Mrs. Eulau, Ms. Perez, Captain Lindsey, Ms. Davis, Mrs. Pekar, and Ms. Dowler—thank you for pushing me to my limits with the pen and encouraging me to pursue my dreams. You have all made a tremendous difference in my life. Finish strong!

There are so many people who have brought me to this point. Alex Castillo, thank you for making me run for student body president—you believed in me when I didn't. You're simply the best and you taught me to fight for what I want, and that fear is the last thing that should hold anyone back. You've got my vote every time.

Eddie Peterson, my Miss Teen California pageant director, you taught me how a golden California girl lives her life. Your engaging smile and generous spirit has brought so much sunshine in my life and to hundreds more. Thanks for showing me my inner sparkle—rhinestones on a crowd will fade but a golden heart never does. To me, you're a 10 every time.

My utmost appreciation to my web designer, Luke Wojnowski—you gave my blog the blowout makeover it needed. Thank you for creating a beautiful website for me and for making me laugh every time I saw you.

A special shout out to the lovely Lisa Bloom who made me *think* through every word, every sentence, and every idea of this book. Thank you for being a yes among so many no's. You are an outstanding woman with all the poise, knowledge, and chutzpah that every girl should have!

To my Chi Omega sisters, thank you so much for encouraging me along the way and for being such a daily reminder of what happiness looks like. You've offered me the most ab-blasting laughs, the most comforting hugs, and the best memories I could ever ask for. I want to especially thank my Big Sister, Kelly Smith, who is one of the most radiant and wise people I know. God blessed me when He put you in my life. Also, thank you to Whitney Heckathorne out in Memphis, Tennessee who has offered endless support in this process—you are a shining star!

Thank you so very much to my amazing editors—both professionals and friends alike. To the talented and gracious Georgia Davis, my first professional editor, I sincerely thank you. You polished and perfected my manuscript and I'm so thankful to Joanna Hyatt for introducing us.

To my best friend since birth, Lauren Beltran. Words cannot express how grateful I am for that day at the pool that created a lifelong friendship. As only children, we've been the sisters we've needed—without all the fighting! From "going down the river in a tootsie roll" to seeing each other graduate, I love you with all my heart. You're as true of a friend as there ever was. Also, thank you so much for all the amazing Sunny Girl pictures you have taken throughout this endeavor (including the cover photo!) and many thanks as well to Travis Christian for designing the cover of the book. You two are quite the dynamic duo!

To my Grandma Joan—you are incredibly smart and I am constantly amazed by your knowledge and more profoundly, your love for family. You have guided our family with grace and I think you are simply exemplary. Now let's get to Ferraro's to celebrate! And a peanut butter and jelly sandwich might be in order as well…*at last*.

Oh to Auntie Nette—where do I begin? From dancing in your nighties as a four-year-old to just sitting and talking for hours, you "get me" better than anyone else. Thank you for your constant encouragement and support. I miss you every day but I love you even more.

To my "dancing" dad—you will always be unforgettable to me. Thank you for showing me what happiness looks like every morning (even if it's at 6:00 am) and thank you for showing me the sunny side in life. You make me laugh more than anyone and you are so well loved by everyone who knows you—especially me.

And to my mom—wow. You are my biggest fan and I am yours. Your enthusiasm for life radiates through all that you do and you have set a shining example for how I should live my life. I'm so glad that we have the relationship we do and I want you to know how sincerely appreciative I am for all of the opportunities you have given me throughout the years. You have given me the best life and I'm so glad that you are here every day to live it with me. I love you more than you know.

And to my portly pet, my dear, beloved Siamese cat, Kiko. Thank you for showing me what true happiness is—a good meal and a nice nap after. You sat, no let me correct myself, you slept with me through every page of this book—thanks for going along on this journey with me.

I hope you all enjoyed the journey just as much as I did.

Sunny Suggested Readings

For Inspiration that Ignites

Channing, W. H., and Mary Engelbreit. *My Symphony*. Kansas City, MO: Andrews McMeel Pub., 1997. Print.

Hay, Louise L. *I Can Do It!: How to Use Affirmations to Change Your Life*. Carlsbad, CA: Hay House, 2009. Print.

Pausch, Randy, and Jeffrey Zaslow. *The Last Lecture*. New York: Hyperion, 2008. Print.

Vujicic, Nick. *Life without Limits: Inspiration for a Ridiculously Good Life*. New York: Doubleday, 2010. Print.

Warren, Richard. *Better Together: What on Earth Are We Here For?* Lake Forest, CA: Purpose Driven, 2004. Print.

Woodburn, Dallas. *3 A.m.: a Collection of Short Stories*. New York: IUniverse, 2005. Print.

Wooden, John, and Don Yaeger. *A Game Plan for Life: the Power of Mentoring*. New York: Bloomsbury USA, 2009. Print.

For Healthy and Happy Living

Aldana, Steven G. *The Culprit & the Cure: Why Lifestyle Is the Culprit behind America's Poor Health and How Transforming That Lifestyle Can Be the Cure*. Mapleton, UT: Maple Mountain, 2005. Print.

Colbert, Don. *The 7 Pillars of Health*. Lake Mary, Fl.: Siloam, 2006. Print.

Etcoff, Nancy L. *Survival of the Prettiest: the Science of Beauty*. New York: Anchor, 2000. Print.

Frankel, Bethenny, and Eve Adamson. *Naturally Thin: Unleash Your Skinnygirl and Free Yourself from a Lifetime of Dieting*. New York: Simon & Schuster, 2009. Print.

Roth, Geneen. *Women Food and God*. New York: Simon & Schuster, 2011. Print.

For Love that Lasts

Argov, Sherry. *Why Men Love Bitches*. Avon, MA: Adams Media, 2009. Print.

Bradbury, Thomas N., and Benjamin R. Karney. *Intimate Relationships*. New York: W.W. Norton &, 2010. Print.

Chapman, Gary D. *The Five Love Languages: How to Express Heartfelt Commitment to Your Mate*. Chicago: Northfield Pub., 2004. Print.

Gray, John S,. *Men Are From Mars: Women Are from Venus*. N.Y.,N.Y: HarperCollins, 1992. Print.

School Suggestions

Kenrick, Douglas T., Steven L. Neuberg, and Robert B. Cialdini. *Social Psychology: Goals in Interaction*. Boston: Allyn & Bacon, 2010. Print.

Lee, Harper. *To Kill a Mockingbird*. New York, NY: Harper, 2010. Print.

Mill, John Stuart, and Colin Heydt. *Utilitarianism*. Peterborough, Ont.: Broadview, 2011. Print.

Pasternack, Lawrence. *Immanuel Kant: Groundwork of the Metaphysics of Morals, in Focus*. London: Routledge, 2002. Print.

Thoreau, Henry D. *Walden: Life in the Woods*. New York: Dodd, Mead &, 1946. Print.

Whitman, Walt, and David S. Reynolds. *Leaves of Grass*. New York: Oxford UP, 2005. Print.

Wolf, Naomi. *The Beauty Myth: How Images of Beauty Are Used against Women*. New York: Perennial, 2002. Print.

For Giving Gratitude

Compton-Rock, Malaak, and Marian Wright. Edelman. *If It Takes a Village, Build One: How I Found Meaning through a Life of Service and 100+ Ways You Can Too*. New York: Broadway, 2010. Print.

Gore, Albert. *Our Choice: a Plan to Solve the Climate Crisis*. Emmaus, PA: Rodale, 2009. Print.

Kidder, Tracy. *Mountains beyond Mountains*. New York: Random House, 2003. Print.

Kinder, Colleen. *Delaying the Real World*. Philadelphia, PA: Running, 2005. Print.

Mortenson, Greg, and David Oliver. Relin. *Three Cups of Tea: One Man's Mission to Promote Peace -- One School at a Time*. New York: Penguin, 2007. Print.

For Stepping Out

Garton, Christie. *U Chic: the College Girl's Guide to Everything*. Naperville, IL: Source, 2009. Print.

Gilbert, Elizabeth. *Eat, Pray, Love: One Woman's Search for Everything across Italy, India and Indonesia*. New York: Viking, 2006. Print.

Schultz, Patricia. *1000 Places to See before You Die*. New York: Workman, 2003. Print.

Schultz, Patricia. *1,000 Places to See in the USA and Canada before You Die*. New York: Workman Pub., 2007. Print.

For Help with Happiness

Bstan-'dzin-rgya-mtsho (Dalai Lama), and Howard C. Cutler. *The Art of Happiness: a Handbook for Living*. New York: Riverhead, 1998. Print.

Gordon, Jon. *The Seed: Finding Purpose and Happiness in Life and Work*. Hoboken, NJ: Wiley, 2011. Print.

O'Connor, Richard. *Happy at Last: the Thinking Person's Guide to Finding Joy*. New York: St. Martin's, 2008. Print.

Rubin, Gretchen Craft. *The Happiness Project: or Why I Spent a Year Trying to Sing in the Morning, Clean My Closets, Fight Right, Read Aristotle, and Generally Have More Fun*. New York, NY: Harper, 2009. Print.

Smith, Ian. *Happy: Simple Steps to Get the Most out of Life*. New York: St. Martin's, 2010. Print.

For Finding Sunny Success

Benson, Peter L., Judy Galbraith, and Pamela Espeland. *What Teens Need to Succeed: Proven, Practical Ways to Shape Your Own Future*. Minneapolis, MN: Free Spirit Pub., 1998. Print.

Bloom, Lisa. *Think: Straight Talk for Women to Stay Smart in a Dumbed down World*. New York: Vanguard, 2011. Print.

Canfield, Jack. *Chicken Soup for the Teen Soul: Real-life Stories by Real Teens*. Deerfield Beach, FL: Health Communications, 2007. Print.

Canfield, Jack, and Kent Healy. *The Success Principles for Teens: How to Get from Where You Are to Where You Want to Be*. Deerfield Beach, FL: Health Communications, 2008. Print.

Canfield, Jack, and Janet Switzer. *The Success Principles: How to Get from Where You Are to Where You Want to Be*. New York: Harper Resource Book, 2005. Print.

Covey, Stephen R. *Living the 7 Habits: Stories of Courage and Inspiration*. New York: Simon & Schuster, 1999. Print.

Sanborn, Mark. *You Don't Need a Title to Be a Leader: How Anyone, Anywhere, Can Make a Positive Difference*. New York: Currency Doubleday, 2006. Print.